MAYDAY

MAYDAY

Nicholas Faith

CHANNEL 4 BOOKS

First published in 1998 by Channel 4 Books,
an imprint of Macmillan Publishers Ltd
25 Eccleston Place, London SW1W 9NF
and Basingstoke

Associated companies throughout the world

ISBN 0 7522 2173 6

9 8 7 6 5 4 3 2 1

A CIP catalogue record for this book is available from
the British Library.

Text design and typesetting by SX Composing DTP, Rayleigh, Essex
Printed and bound in Great Britain by
Mackays of Chatham plc, Chatham, Kent
Plate section design by Roger Lightfoot

Plate Section Picture Acknowledgements: page 1, all pictures (Illustrated London
News Picture Library); page 2 top (Rex Features Ltd), bottom (PA News Photo
Library); page 3 top (Rex Features Ltd), bottom (Rex Features Ltd/Dagbladet/Sipa
Press); page 4 (Associated Press PRESSFOTO); page 5 top (Associated Press
WEST AUSTRALIAN), bottom (PA News Photo Library); page 6 top (Rex
Features Ltd/Sipa Press), bottom left (Rex Features Ltd/Sipa Press), bottom right
(Rex Features Ltd); page 7 top (PA News Photo Library), bottom (Rex Features
Ltd); page 8 top (Associated Press), bottom (Associated Press AP).

This book accompanies the television series 'Mayday'
made by Darlow Smithson for Channel 4.
Executive producer: John Smithson
Producer: Greg Lanning

For my grandsons, Seán, Frankie and Jack – in the hope that they won't have too many nautical (mis)adventures.

Contents

Acknowledgements

This is the third 'disaster' book I've written and I grow increasingly amazed at the competence and the helpfulness of everyone involved. At Boxtree Katy Carrington remains a complete brick, Hazel Orme the swiftest, most professional – and most encouraging – of editors, while Jan Surtees, Nicky Ryde and Daphne Walsh manage to transcribe masses of interviews with often inarticulate witnesses and officials into intelligible English to provide me with the essential framework for the book. There is also one author I would like to single out: Norman Hooke, whose book, *Maritime Disasters, 1963–1996* has proved invaluable.

But to me even more astonishing has been the help given by the team at Darlow Smithson, producers of 'Mayday', all up to their eyes in work, but none of them ever too busy to help me with my – often naive – enquiries. Thank you: John Smithson, David Darlow, Greg Lanning, Jonathan Jones, Philip K. Wearne, Caroline Hecks, Emma Jessop and Rebecca Mulraine.

Introduction

Exitio est avidum mare nautis
The greedy sea is there to be a doom for sailors
                                        Horace

I have to confess to what might be described as a not inconsiderable dread of the sea. All my sympathies go out to the mythical Greek sailor who took up his oar and trudged inland until he found a spot where no one knew what it was. But, like many other confirmed landlubbers, I retain an enormous, if horrified, fascination for the terrors that lurk not just on the mighty ocean but even on the most apparently innocuous stretch of water.

This fascination is almost universal. Historically, I think, it is due to the wide variety of problems associated with the sea, how impossible it is to know it in any depth – both literally and figuratively – and, above all, because of the immense number of extraordinary stories associated with it. The sea has always provided innumerable examples of two of the funda-mental ingredients in many stories: the battle of man against nature; and the almost limitless number of ways in which man can behave in extreme situations.

This book, like the television series it accompanies, is concerned only with a small selection of the hundreds of marine accidents that have occurred since 1945. They have been chosen to illustrate some of the more important dangers that have arisen because of the ever-growing size of ships, the most dangerous type of ship, and the damage, environmental as well as human, that can be caused by the present pattern of shipping activity. I hope that both series and book will help to awaken the public to the needless dangers facing sea-goers that result from the present chaotic regulatory situation.

The book does not cover the appalling results of wars at sea or their

1

legacy, the minefields that continue to take their toll, especially in the waters of the Persian Gulf. It would, perhaps, be a fitting additional tribute to Princess Diana's campaign against landmines if a similar effort were mounted to remove the minefields that pollute the world's seas. Wartime losses from the sinking of individual ships are greater than those suffered in peacetime. British and American readers will probably be familiar with the sinking by a German U-boat in 1915 of the *Lusitania*, an event that did much to bring the USA into the First World War. There were similar, though less well publicized horrors in the Second World War, like the sinking, also by German submarines, of the *Athenia* and the *City of Benares*.

But the record for the loss of life from a single disaster stems from the little-known operation nicknamed the 'German Dunkirk' in the spring of 1945 when over two million German nationals fleeing from the Russians were carried from ports in Poland and East Prussia to the relative safety of West Germany, where they fell into the hands of the more merciful American and British armies. But there was a price to pay: in just under eleven weeks almost 18,000 Germans were drowned in three separate sinkings while they were on their way back to the fatherland. The worst single disaster in the history of maritime disasters was that of the liner *Wilhelm Gustloff*, which was carrying 8,000 passengers when it was torpedoed by a Russian submarine on 30 January 1945. Seven thousand of those on board drowned immediately and many others died of hypothermia after being rescued from the icy sea. Just ten days later the German liner *General Steuben* was torpedoed by the same submarine, killing 3,000 refugees, while another, the *Goya*, was sunk on 16 April, killing virtually all of the 7,000 persons aboard.

Yet, for passengers as well as sailors, things had been infinitely worse in the past. As Bella Bathurst wrote,*

> Two hundred years ago, almost half of all British seamen died
> pursuing their trade, either killed by the punishing life on board ship
> or sacrificed to storms and drownings. During the Napoleonic wars,
> it was reckoned that, quite apart from those lost in battle, over five
> thousand British sailors died every year from the force of nature.
> The horrors this produced can be seen at its most vivid in Turner's

Sea-towers, Granta 61, The Sea, London, 1998.

great painting *Slaves Throwing Overboard the Dead and Dying – Typhoon Coming In.*

Ships and sailing continue to get safer. If you go back to the immediate post-war era, most of the world's cargo ships consisted either of pre-war vessels, or the thousands of Liberty ships, all-purpose cargo vessels mass-produced by the Americans during the Second World War. They were designed only to last until the end of the war, but many were virtually given away to Greek ship-owners to help compensate for their wartime losses and sailed the seas for a generation or more after 1945. Worse were the T2s, the tanker equivalent of the Liberty ships. In 1963 the judge in a New York court said that they had proved 'unreliable to say the least': by mid-1946 fifteen had sustained major fractures. To make matters worse, ship-owners had then tried to rebuild them as bulk carriers – the judge's remarks were made after the mysterious disappearance of the *Marine Sulphur Queen*, which, he said, was obviously unseaworthy because 'the owners had totally disregarded the most elementary rules of ship construction' while they were converting her.

Wartime construction was generally shoddy. When the bulk carrier *Marine Electric* capsized and sank off the coast of Virginia in February 1963, 'the wastage of the hatch covers and deck plating had reached such a point that the crew was patching the numerous holes with epoxy and using waterproof tape for securing the hatches'.* Worse, according to the chief mate, the patches wouldn't stay on 'and there were many holes with no patches at all'. When he kicked one of the hatch covers, 'I kicked off a piece of paint and another hole showed up'.

Yet although life at sea is infinitely safer than it was even fifty years ago, it is still dangerous – largely because of the continuing incapacity of the international maritime community to put its house in order and impose elementary regulations that would save thousands of lives every year. Moreover, the possibility of danger increases every year because the world's fleet is growing, from 130 million gross tons in 1960 to 508 million in 1996. Of course, ships are getting bigger so this does not represent a proportional increase in numbers; but bigger does not necessarily mean safer, although the number of accidents, in British waters, anyway, has not changed greatly either way – about two thousand incidents are reported every year.

*R. A. Cahill, *Collisions and Their Causes*, Fair Play Publications, London, 1983.

Given the ever-increasing number of ships, this represents some sort of progress (similarly, car accidents have not increased as fast as the number of cars on the road). As so often is the case with shipping, no overall figures are available but Mark Dickinson, of the International Transport Federation (ITF),* reckons that mining is not, as is generally thought, the most dangerous industry in the world: 'It's fisheries, followed very closely by the shipping industry. We estimate that on average every year, over two thousand seafarers will lose their lives due to accidents on board and through maritime casualties as well.'

As it is, maritime transport remains far less effectively regulated than air travel, or the world's railway systems. Again and again, while researching and writing this book, I kept thinking back to the similar research I had done on air accidents for my previous book *Black Box*, and reflecting on the contrast between the two types of travel: the one, by air, infinitely more dangerous in theory, infinitely better policed, and therefore, if not safer, at least more protective of the lives of passengers and crew than the maritime community.

It helps the cause of aviation safety that air travel is perceived to be so dangerous and that the skies are dominated by the products of two major aircraft manufacturers, the American Boeing and the European Airbus, and by aircraft flying under the flags of major industrialized countries. It makes a stark contrast to the anarchy of life on the ocean wave.

In the airline industry, investigations are compulsory and serious. Investigations and inspection of ships are haphazard, most effectively regulated by the world's marine insurers in the absence of any properly working international system. The classification societies they employ are of varying quality, and a useful first step towards safe seas would be to increase the existing pressure on the societies to take responsibility for any disasters suffered by ships they have inspected.

The international body concerned with marine safety, the International Maritime Organization (IMO), proceeds by consensus, with progress in safety matters dictated by the pace of the slowest ship in the convoy. 'The maritime community has global regulations,' says trade unionist Mark Dickinson, 'but their weakness is that they're enforced locally. They are

*A federation of five hundred affiliated trade unions from all over the world representing five million transport workers in all branches of the transport industry.

4

enforced nationally by sovereign governments who are allowed to register ships.' One of the answers, says Admiral John Lang, of Britain's Maritime Accidents Investigation Branch (MAIB), is greater powers 'to access evidence held by some foreign entity. I can think of instances where a vital bit of equipment is locked up in some magistrate's court overseas and we can't get hold of it until their investigation is complete. That does inhibit us in getting to the bottom of some particular accident.

'If there's been a collision and the other ship was a foreign flag vessel manned by foreign nationalities in international waters, or in somebody else's territorial seas, there are quite considerable difficulties in talking to those people if they do not wish to be interviewed. That means that you've only got half the story and that is obviously unsatisfactory.'

Progress is hampered by the vested interests opposed to any change that might cost money, notably the so-called 'flags of convenience' countries, like Liberia, Panama, the Bahamas and Cyprus, which provide registration for ship-owners anxious to minimize costs, both in the construction of their ships and the qualifications (and nationality) of their crews. It does not help that the Greeks, still one of the world's major maritime nations, are fiercely independent, deeply reluctant to submit to any form of external discipline and most ingenious in avoiding any restrictions imposed from outside on their commercial and operational freedom. The unhappy results of what could be described as the splendid Greek entrepreneurial tradition are visible in most of the chapters of this book, for unfortunately shipping was the first industry to be globalized and, as a result, the seas are only too free. Not surprisingly, says Mark Dickinson, 'over the last fifty years national ship-owners employing national crews and regulated by national maritime authorities started flagging out to countries like Liberia, Panama, Honduras', which now account for half the world's ocean-going shipping in tonnage terms.

The main reason for using flags of convenience is to reduce the costs of crewing. In addition ship-owners can save enormous sums – estimated at $1 million, in an OECD (Organization for Economic Cooperation and Development) report published in 1997 – in registration and inspection charges. 'A ship-owner who wants to save money and avoid detection,' says Dickinson, 'has a good chance of getting away with it. One of the main attractions is the lack of effective enforcement by flag-of-convenience states. They don't have the infrastructure, they don't have the expertise, and they don't have the political will to enforce internationally agreed rules on the ships under their register. They can't do this for one basic reason: ship-owners have no attachment whatsoever to the flag states and you don't have any way of penalizing them for breaking the rules.'

The result is that every time a ship registered under a flag of convenience enters the ports, or the waters, of an industrialized country – which happens hundreds if not thousands of times every day – it brings with it many of the worst aspects of the Third World: its working conditions, its lack of concern for safety, training, discipline and, in many cases, mutual comprehension. As John Lang says, 'The crews of many of the vessels involved in disasters are inexperienced novices, drawn from many different countries. They do not necessarily have a grasp of the language used in the safety instructions – or, indeed, by the ship's own officers'. When the ill-fated *Scandinavian Star** suffered her first disastrous fire, the crew were of nine different nationalities but none spoke French, a major handicap because all the ship's safety instructions were in that language.

The absence of control can also involve appalling working conditions. Dickinson explains: 'We have cases of seafarers who have been locked up in their own cabins when in port, to prevent them going ashore and telling any-body about the problems that they're experiencing. We have examples of seafarers who have been starving because there's no food on board, ships arriving with basically just bags of rice and undrinkable water. We have examples of seafarers who have not been paid for eighteen months and these are part of the routine caseload within this organization.'

Inevitably disasters result, often from the professional inadequacy of those in charge of the ship. After the sinking of the tanker *Aegean Captain* following her collision with another tanker, the *Atlantic Empress*, in July 1979, spilling 270,000 tonnes of oil, in its report the Board of Investigation remarked, 'It is an arresting fact that a laden VLCC,† with a large crew and female and infant supernumeraries on board, should be proceeding into the dusk in the charge of an uncertified watch-keeper, a radio officer who was being paid to double as a deck officer, who was known to be a habitual drunkard and who on this occasion was affected by alcohol recently taken in the opinion of the able seaman who stood the watch with him.'

*See Chapter 6.
†Very Large Crude Carrier.

But it is too easy to blame the master or crew. Just as in air crashes the pilot is blamed or in railway accidents the engine driver, so it is with the crew of a ship when a disaster has occurred. Dickinson puts it bluntly: 'I think it's often the case in casualty investigations that they look for the weakest link and the weakest link is already a seafarer who's dead. He can't answer back, can't tell you what actually happened.'

Too often the master is second-guessed, with disastrous results, by his shore-based superiors. This happens increasingly often as international communications become more sophisticated. 'There have been instances,' says John Lang, 'where a master finds his ship is in trouble, obviously takes whatever action is needed to correct it, but rather than perhaps call for help by issuing a Mayday signal feels inclined to ring up his owners on satellite telephone to find out what he should be doing next. That will often delay the appropriate salvage action which needs to be taken. In my opinion owners must support the master in his actions.' But the owners – and the companies chartering these ships – are in a hurry. There is, says John Lang, an 'implacable pressure on the crews of ships to cut corners, to "sail too close to the wind" – or too close to other ships or to notorious danger spots for commercial reasons, to deliver their cargo, or their passengers on time'. There seems little that can be done to reduce this effect of competition except to repeat the adage, more common in the aviation industry, that it is 'better to be five minutes late in this world than twenty years early in the next'.

It would also be too easy to say piously, 'Ah, yes, most of these problems stem from international capitalist practices, from the globalization practised at sea long before it hit the business schools.' But there's a much more brutal force in action here, which I call the 'small earthquake in Chile' syndrome: the lack of interest among the Western media – and the public they serve – in dramatic events, however great the loss of life, that do not involve their own countrymen. I doubt if one reader in a hundred has heard of the Philippine ferry, the *Doña Paz*, which sank off Manila in 1987 with the loss of at least 4,235 souls – far and away the biggest loss of life in a single maritime disaster in peacetime.

The lack of interest in such events, let alone in the regular loss of life among the crews of hundreds of cargo vessels sunk every year – virtually all of whom come from the Third World or from Eastern Europe – forms a stark contrast to the intense interest in such horrors as the sinking of the ferries *Herald of Free Enterprise* and the *Estonia,* which involved European casualties.* Oil spills, too, cause public outcry: they kill birds and sea-life – but they rarely involve loss of human life and their effects have proved temporary. The consciousness of the Western public badly needs to be raised if any effective international action is to be taken to reduce the conditions that lead to the persistent and unnecessary loss of life at sea.

Public awareness is the only route into the closed world of shipping, because probably the biggest single problem is its insularity, its lack of input from consumers – except when a major disaster, which could probably have been prevented, occurs. When Torbjorn Kalberg and some of his fellow survivors from the *Scandinavian Star* demonstrated at the annual meeting of the International Maritime Organization (IMO) the delegates were outraged. What they should have been discussing, says Kalberg, is that 'The shipping industry should be forced to realize that their activities on board the ships should be taken more seriously and that they should accept being criticized, like any other business, by people not necessarily belonging to their own circles. I think to this day they have not accepted this. In land-based industries you have to accept meddling from other people. These people from the maritime organizations, they're not having to associate with people from other branches of life.'

The Americans are trying now to impose some minimum standards on the ships that call at their ports. The same effort applied by Japan and the European Union would banish potentially lethal vessels from international waters. It would also help if major oil companies were pressured to ensure that they chartered only tankers that conformed to the highest standards of construction and that were manned by properly qualified crews. But, until Europeans or Japanese are killed by one in a tanker disaster, that is unlikely.

*See Chapter 3.

1
Never Again: the *Titanic* and After

The Olympics were conceived, proposed, planned and built by a man
[Lord Pirrie], who lived beyond his dreams and would stop at nothing
to promote himself and his beloved shipyard when it fell victim to a
cash-flow crisis. He unleashed a rapacious J. P. Morgan on an unprepared Britain and helped to sell his own principal customer down the
river. The latter, the White Star line, had a record of dubious business
ethics and slap-happy seamanship. Its hereditary chief was a weak
character and White Star's commodore was not just a showman who
made the passengers feel good but also a show-off, who drove the
world's biggest liners as if they were gigantic speedboats.

Robin Gardiner and Dan Van der Vat*

After that introduction it seems surprising not that the *Titanic*, one of the
Olympic class, struck an iceberg but that any ships of that class managed to
sail anywhere without accident. Yet the shock of the disaster remains as
fresh as ever. Today, eighty-six years after the allegedly unsinkable *Titanic*
disappeared beneath the waves of the Atlantic, a film of the disaster has
proved easily the most successful to date in the history of motion pictures.
That in itself is astonishing, for the key to most successful movies is the element of suspense – and the only unknown element in the 1998 movie is
whether the hero will survive.

The fascination with the minuscule details of the disaster remains
unabated, the appetite for discussion apparently insatiable. I found myself
caught up in earnest discussions with friends as to whether Captain
Walter Lord of the *Californian*, the ship nearest to the *Titanic*, knew about
the liner's plight. And even today passengers on the world's largest liner,
the *QE2*, insist on peering over the side when she goes out of her way to

*In *The Riddle of the Titanic*, Orion, London, 1995 – a most stimulating read.

pass over the graveyard of the *Titanic*, three hundred miles off New-foundland.

The interest is not purely morbid, for the disaster was one of the key events of the twentieth century. Far more than fifteen hundred lives were lost and a shipping line was condemned. Coming, as it did, two years before the outbreak of the First World War, the tragedy marked the end of an era in which progress – technical, financial, scientific, commercial, industrial – seemed certain, unstoppable, unchallengeable, and exposed every flaw in the social and industrial structure that had been built since the battle of Waterloo. If the pride of British shipping – and the liner's name alone dis-tilled the pride and arrogance of the times – could be shown to be flawed in her operation as much as in her construction, then the world was a far less secure place than anyone had imagined. When the *Titanic* foundered, the passengers were so persuaded that she was unsinkable that many refused to clamber into the lifeboats: it seemed safer to stay on board a ship that would never go to the bottom.

It is easy to assert that the disaster showed the rot that had begun to eat at the foundations of Britain's assumed supremacy, symbolized by the size and power of the Royal Navy and of the country's merchant fleet. But the continuing fascination with the *Titanic* also lies in the fact that the story has all the ingredients of a lasting legend: human frailty, heroes and villains, the wide variations of human behaviour in extreme conditions, and the conclu-sion that a complex series of coincidences had to take place for such a major disaster to occur.

It is such a fascinating subject that most of us can find an element in it that continues to disturb us. In my case it is the fact that in 1898 an American mystic, Morgan Robertson, and former merchant-navy officer, understood the danger presented by icebergs to the ever-larger, ever-faster liners of the period and published a novella called *Futility*. It described how a liner called *Titan*, of much the same capacity, size and description as the *Titanic*, hit an iceberg – on the same, starboard side as the *Titanic* – and sank.

Many of the causes of subsequent disasters first emerged into the full glare of international publicity with the *Titanic*. The captain and his boss, the chairman of the shipping line, were preoccupied with speed and punctuality. The crew didn't know each other, and many were relatively unacquainted with the ship. Rescue efforts were bungled in a welter of misunderstandings due to poor communications. And the disaster itself was marked by a mixture of heroism, selfishness and contradictory impressions as to how everyone involved really did behave.

To me, possibly the most extraordinary and generally under-emphasized element in the story is that of the White Star line itself. 'Living on the edge,' wrote Gardiner and Van der Vat, 'whether of ruin or the latest shipping development, was essential to the ethos of the White Star line throughout its unhappy history.'

It was founded in 1845. The accidents in which its ships before the *Titanic* went under included the worst peacetime mercantile accident ever previously recorded when the *Atlantic* sank off the Canadian coast in March 1873, killing at least 546 people through the incompetence and recklessness of the captain. In 1868 the cattle-steamer *Naronic*, at over 6,500 tons the largest cargo ship in the world, disappeared. Six years later the liner *Germanic* sank under the weight of the ice on its upper decks while in New York harbour.* As Van der Vat and Gardiner put it, the line's list of disasters 'stood out even among the vicissitudes of the many companies that suffered marine casualties over the turn of the century'.

In 1902, after half a century of financial disaster and share manipulation, White Star was sold to J. Pierpont Morgan by Bruce Ismay, the rather weak son of Thomas Henry Ismay, who had fought to keep his line out of Morgan's hands.† The American financier, who had already created 'trusts' that virtually eliminated competition in other industries, most obviously steel, was trying to do the same with the large, glamorous, profitable business of transatlantic travel by building up a group, the International Merchant Marine Company (IMM). This would bring together British and German shipping lines and crush the Cunard company, standard-bearer of British supremacy on the Atlantic run.

In response, the British government ensured that Cunard benefited from cheap loans to enable it to build three super-liners, first the *Lusitania* and the *Mauretania*, then the *Aquitania*, completed in 1914. They were all advanced ships, their shape the result of a series of scientific studies as to

*It was refloated and survived, ultimately in Turkish livery, until 1950. Only the Cunard line's *Parthia*, which lived to eighty-six, had a longer sea-going record.
†Morgan declined to travel on the *Titanic* because of alleged illness. After the disaster he was found at Baden-Baden taking the waters in the company of a French mistress.

hull form. The *Mauretania* held the Blue Riband, the unofficial transatlantic speed record, for over twenty years, while the rather slower *Aquitania* was much loved by travellers because she was so stable. In response, Morgan was persuaded to finance three new monsters, the *Olympic*, the *Britannic* and the *Titanic*, all bigger than their British-owned rivals. The siren voice was that of William James Pirrie, chairman of the cash-strapped Harland and Wolff shipyard in Belfast, and a director of both White Star and IMM. (Pirrie's career was unaffected by the wreck of the *Titanic*. Before he died – at sea – in 1924, he had become Viscount Pirrie.) Morgan, Pirrie and Ismay were not the sort of people who put customers, or safety, before their own financial interests – and, of course, the tie-up between the three meant that, unlike the close supervision exercised by Cunard over its suppliers, Harland and Wolff went its own way virtually uncontrolled. Moreover, White Star had no experience of building fast ships; they had relied on comfort to attract passengers in the past.

Like all White Star ships, the *Titanic* was built at Harland and Wolff's yard. Her design was a major factor in the disaster: unlike Cunard's ships she didn't have a watertight deck connecting all the bulkheads (and the Cunarders also had a double bottom, rising eight feet up the side of the ship). The *Titanic* had supposedly 'watertight bulkheads', which did not reach to the top of the hull. In the event, water and ice could spill over from one compartment to another; once four compartments were filled, the water would slop over, like that in an overfilled ice tray, ensuring the ship's destruction. Famously, the original design, which would have ensured that there were enough lifeboats for all the passengers, was changed – to preserve the sleekness of the ship's lines and to ensure that she would go that little bit faster and thus compete with the new Cunarders, the 'greyhounds of the Atlantic'.

The key to the disaster, though, was human: Captain E. J. Smith, the ship's master. By the standards of the time he was elderly. When he took command of the *Titanic* he was a white-bearded sixty-two-year-old with an approach to navigation that can be described either as dashing or reckless. 'He used to make us flush with pride,' said one of his officers, as he navigated in tight corners 'with only a matter of feet to spare between each end of the ship and the banks'. Over the course of his long sea-going career he gathered an appalling record of accidents. Under him, three liners grounded and he had three accidents in a year in command of the *Titanic*'s sister, the

Olympic: she trapped and nearly crushed a tug on her maiden voyage, collided with a British cruiser and ran over a wreck, losing a propeller blade in the process.

During the last hours of the *Titanic* Smith's cavalier attitude was demonstrated with startling, and tragic, clarity. He was not helped by the lack of binoculars for the lookouts. There has been a mysterious exchange of officers between the *Titanic* and the *Olympic* and the key to the locker containing them had been left behind. Without binoculars, not only had the lookouts no help in spotting icebergs but in icy weather they were denied protection for their eyes; they were high on a ship doing 22 knots in a freezing wind. One of the lookouts, Frederick Fleet, later claimed, almost certainly correctly, that with binoculars he would have seen the iceberg in time to save the ship.

Yet they, and above all the master, should have known the conditions: six warnings of ice in the area had been received. One had been given by Captain Smith to Bruce Ismay, who passed it much later to the officer on the bridge, probably in an effort to ensure that the ship did not slow down (at the inquiry Ismay claimed that he had forgotten about it). The wireless operator received one from the steamer *Mesaba* but didn't pass it on to the bridge because he was too busy dealing with messages from passengers. Finally, only a couple of hours before the disaster, the liner received two warnings from a nearby cargo ship ('have just passed through heavy field ice and several icebergs') and the *Californian* ('we are stopped and surrounded by ice'). But still the jaunty Captain Smith ploughed ahead at full speed. As he had so often before, he cut corners.

Even after the collision, when an inspection below deck had convinced those in charge that the ship was doomed, it was twenty minutes before the first lifeboat was lowered into the water. Lifeboat drills had been cancelled and no one was ready for such an unthinkable emergency. (Neither were the lifeboats: many lacked lights, water and other basic necessities.)

When the ship was abandoned, chaos ensued: there were too few lifeboats and the ship's officers did not realize that those they had could take many more people than clambered to safety in them. Some were launched with only twenty-five aboard, half their capacity. However, even if they had been full to capacity, only 200 out of the 1,522 who were lost might have been saved.

How many of these would have been from the third-class accommodation is another matter. As was dramatically illustrated in James Cameron's film, over half the women and children and six out of seven men in third class died largely because no systematic search of the ship was made after the collision; they had further to go to reach the upper decks and safety, and were restrained from doing so by class-conscious officers. Virtually all of the women and children in first class survived, but less than a third of the men.

The last word on the *Titanic* should perhaps be left to that former master mariner, the novelist Joseph Conrad, who understood the anguish of those who go down to 'the sea that plays with men till their hearts are broken, and wears stout ships to death'. In a private printed pamphlet 'Some Reflections on the Splendid Enquiry Into the Loss of the Titanic', he poured scorn on every aspect of the ship itself, the shipping line and its directors. The famous watertight compartments? 'She was not divided. You and I, and our little boys, when we want to divide, say, a box, we take good care to procure a piece of wood which will reach from the bottom to the lid. We know that if it does not reach all the way up the box will not be divided into two compartments. It will be only partly divided.' The delusion that increased size was progress? If that were so then 'elephantiasis, which causes a man's legs to become as large as tree-trunks, would be a sort of progress.' The 'big ship isn't a servant of progress in any sense. She is the servant of commercialism. For progress, if dealing with the problems of a material world, has some sort of moral aspect. Bigness [alone] is mere exaggeration.' The suggestion, made by a White Star director, that everything would have been fine if the liner had met the iceberg head-on inspired magnificent scorn:

> The proper handling of an unsinkable ship, you see, will demand that she should be made to hit the iceberg very accurately with her nose, because should you perchance scrape the bluff of the bow instead, she may, without ceasing to be as unsinkable as before, find her way to the bottom. I congratulate the future transatlantic passengers on the new and vigorous sensations in store for them. They shall go bounding across from iceberg to iceberg at 25 knots with precision and safety, and a 'cheerful bumping sound' as the immortal poem has it.

The insufficient lifeboats? 'If you can't get more boats, then sell less tickets. Don't drown so many people on the finest, calmest night that was ever known in the North Atlantic – even if you have provided them with a little music to get drowned by.' And of money raised to help the relatives of the band, Conrad's response was:

> I, who am not a sentimentalist, think it would have been finer if the band of the *Titanic* had been quietly saved, instead of being drowned while playing – whatever tune they were playing, poor devils. I would rather they had been saved to support their families than to see their families supported by the magnificent generosity of the subscribers.

In the welter of inquiries on both sides of the Atlantic that followed the disaster, all sorts of official inadequacies emerged. Most importantly, the Board of Trade, the British government department responsible for maritime safety, had not adjusted its regulations on ship construction since the first large liner, of above 10,000 tons, had been launched two decades before the *Titanic*. Its inaction had been due to complacency for, like everyone else, it had assumed that the latest liners were virtually unsinkable.

Following the *Titanic* disaster not only did the Board revise its regulations and inspection systems, but in 1914 the world's seafaring countries adopted the SOLAS rules – Safety of Lives At Sea. These were and are administered by the International Maritime Organization. From time to time – but only four times in all, the last in 1974 – they are revised and updated. Although the new regulations introduced in the two years following the sinking of the *Titanic* proved inadequate, disasters involving massive loss of life became relatively few and far between.

For fifty years afterwards only a handful of peacetime maritime accidents seized the public's imagination. One was the fire on board the American liner *Morro Castle* in 1934, and this was not so much because 124 passengers and crew died in the blaze but because the affair was shrouded in mystery. The characters in a drama far more complex than that of the *Titanic* were headed by Captain Robert Willmott, a heavy-set, florid-faced fifty-six-year-old. The chief officer, William F. Warms, had worked his way up from cabin boy, despite a couple of incidents in which his neglect of fire and lifeboat drills had led to his suspension. He hated the chief engineer, Eban Abbott, whom he described as a 'stuffed tailor's dummy in the engine room', while Abbott referred to Warms as 'that worm on the bridge'. If anything, the situation was worse in the radio department where the chief operator, George Rogers, was successfully plotting against the man whose place he had taken, George Alagna. Willmott suspected Rogers of plotting against him too and vowed to sack him when the ship returned to New York after her next round trip to Havana. There were, seemingly, no end of tensions in a genuinely unhappy ship, which was full of suspected 'Communist agitators' – the usual description of anyone demanding better pay or conditions during the Depression when ship-owners felt free to exploit their employees.

Some months before the disaster Captain Willmott, a nervous soul, had become violently ill after a meal that he suspected contained poison. On this trip he had been warned of a bottle of sulphuric acid on board, which Rogers had taken away from Alagna. On the last night of the ship's regular voyage from Havana to New York, Willmott was taken ill after eating a slice of melon and died. The next day, as the ship was approaching New York, fire broke out in a locker in the writing room and, in a ship full of varnished wood, spread rapidly. In the confusion, more than a quarter of the passengers died. The disaster led to a series of inquiries – and arrests. Suspicions of sabotage and foul play were rife, made even stronger by the captain's death just before the fire.

At their trials, Warms was accused of neglect and professional misconduct for his failure to take charge properly, while Abbott was universally condemned for having lost his head and left the ship at the first opportunity. They were both sent to prison, and Henry Ecabaud, the executive vice-president of the company that owned the *Morro Castle* the Ward Line, received a suspended prison sentence. At a subsequent appeal, Warms was exonerated, but while Abbott's behaviour was condemned the court could not find him guilty of any particular crime and he was released.

At the centre of the mystery was George Rogers. At first he had played a starring role as 'the operator who had stayed at his post until the last minute' but his later life proved him to be a real criminal. It soon transpired that the 'heroic' Rogers was a sociopath manipulator. In the late 1930s he was convicted of the attempted murder of a detective with a bomb he had devised, while in 1953 he murdered an elderly couple who had befriended him. He died in prison in 1958. Perhaps he was also responsible, if not for the fire, at least for the murder of the unfortunate Captain Willmott.

The *Morro Castle* was a purely American mystery. More widespread shock was generated by the sinking of the splendid Italian liner *Andrea Doria* off Long Island in 1956 after she collided with the Swedish liner *Stockholm*, even though 'only' forty-seven lives were lost, all but three from the Italian liner. The shock was greater because the 29,000-ton *Andrea Doria* was a beautiful vessel, the first to be built in Italy after 1945 and a magnificent example of Italian style and elegance.

About 150 miles from the Nantucket Light Vessel, which lies outside the approaches to New York harbour, the liner ran into patchy fog, which was not unusual for the time of year. Under those conditions, mariners are advised to proceed only at a 'moderate' speed, but the master, Captain Calamai, was anxious to reach New York on time the next day and reduced speed by only a single knot to 21 knots.

The *Stockholm* had just left New York and was sailing in the opposite direction in clear weather, only a few miles west of the *Andrea Doria*, before she ran into the fog bank – and the Italian liner. At the time most of the blame fell on the unfortunate Captain Calamai. He indeed saw the Swedish ship on his radar screen and broke the rule of the maritime road by not turning automatically to starboard to avoid collision. In his hurry to get to New York, Captain Calamai had not tried to stop his ship until too late. Ironically, if he had been going at full speed the collision would never have occurred: he would have avoided the *Stockholm* altogether. Also, he had never had any formal instruction in the use of radar – hence the sick joke that it was the first 'radar-assisted collision'.

But some authorities, including Richard A. Cahill,* an experienced navigator, have asserted that the primary fault lay with the *Stockholm*. First, the captain ignored the recommendation made in 1948 to separate west- and eastbound tracks in the crowded sea lanes off New York, saying that his employers were not party to the agreement and that adhering to it would have added two hours to his sailing time. More importantly, the youthful third officer of the *Stockholm*, Johan-Ernst Carstens, who had been left in charge of the bridge, made several mistakes in the long interval – twenty-five minutes – between the time when the *Andrea Doria* first showed up on the *Stockholm*'s radar screen and the collision itself. It seems that he had miscalculated the course of the two ships and that he had therefore ordered the *Stockholm* to turn to starboard, bringing her directly across the bows of the Italian liner. During the approach, however, he had plenty of time to call the master to the bridge and, in Cahill's eyes at least, his major error was to try

*In *Collisions and Their Causes*, op. cit.

to go it alone. As Cahill puts it, 'Carstens probably fell into the commonest trap of all. He let his pride overrule his judgement.'

Despite last-minute evasive action, the ships were heading for each other at a combined speed of 40 knots, thus giving too little time to avoid the collision. The bow of the *Stockholm* hit the starboard side of the *Andrea Doria* just after midnight on 26 July. Although the bows of the Swedish liner were pushed back about 60 feet she remained afloat because the forward bulkhead held fast and contained the damage. But the *Doria* had been damaged in the starboard fuel tanks. These were nearly empty so the water rushed in; the port tanks were empty and provided no balance for the ship, which promptly started to list so badly to starboard that only half the lifeboats – those on the starboard side – could be launched. Even when they were lowered they were a long way out from the hull and had to be braced into the side of the ship, which caused considerable delay in launching them. Chaos followed as the boats had to be loaded from the stern of the ship. The first three to reach the *Stockholm* were only half full and contained mostly stewards and galley staff.

Fortunately, one of the thirty ships that rushed to the scene was the giant French liner the *Ile de France*: she arrived while there were still 1,500 people on the *Doria* out of the 1,700 who had originally sailed with her. Most were saved. Early the next morning the *Doria* sank, saluted by the *Ile de France* which circled the spot where she had foundered, sounded her siren, set her colours at half-mast and dipped the ensign in salute to a great ship.

In the aftermath of the collision, captains were advised to fill empty fuel tanks with sea-water to maintain buoyancy, which they had been loath to do for fear of contamination. Since then, improved radar – and instruction in its use – has helped to prevent any such disaster to a major ocean liner in the past forty years.

2
Bulk Carriers, Bulk Losses

The sea will find the problem. If there's any weakness there, bad weather invariably catches it out. It's a lesson we should have learned from Noah onwards, but it has to be relearned time and time and time again. Seamen are dying because of this problem.

Lancelot Bedlington

Of all the types of ship sailing the seas possibly the most vulnerable is the bulk carrier used to transport coal, grain, iron ore and other bulky raw materials. These ships are peculiarly vulnerable for a variety of reasons. 'A lot of these bulk carriers,' says Professor Douglas Faulkner, who investigated the loss of the *Derbyshire*, 'are very old, their sides get rusted and most of them have single-skin sides. When the ships get rusted they start breaking. The water comes into the hold and the ship starts sinking.'

These carriers, especially the smaller ones, have become the modern equivalents of the tramps with their 'salt-caked smokestacks' of John Masefield's day before the First World War, and attract the dodgier operators. As a result, the casualty figures are horrifying. Between 1973 and 1996, 375 bulk carriers were lost, fifteen every year. The figures exclude a dozen or more lost in war conditions, mostly in the Persian Gulf during the Iran–Iraq War of the early 1980s. Typically, in the first seven years of the 1980s, 151 bulk carriers were written off as total losses. Only thirty-eight had sunk because of bad weather when either the ship broke in two or sustained a severe battering that led to leakage or fracture of the hull. The pattern of ownership gives a clue as to the reasons for the high rate of loss: of the 375 ships lost, 223 were registered in only four countries – Liberia, Cyprus (with 19 losses in the years 1990–96 alone), Panama and, above all, Greece with 73 losses, nearly a fifth of the total.

Ironically, says Faulkner, the bigger the carrier, the more vulnerable, and their weaknesses are liable more often to be fatal: 'In the really stormy seas, the smaller ship, providing her watertight integrity is good, will survive a great deal of punishment, and she'll ride up and over waves. The big ships have to tunnel through them and it's that which causes a high pressure on the structure. You have these big old open-hold ships with vulnerable sides and hatch-covers, and poor maintenance. It means that they are much more likely to experience water ingress than other ships may be.'

The main underlying problem with all bulk carriers is corrosion, which over the years may reduce thick steel to a wafer-thin slice. Other problems include poor welding construction. Strain is placed on these vessels by the sheer weight of the cargo but also the loading methods and 'cargo shift'. Loading, especially from modern coal or iron-ore terminals, can be incredibly fast – up to 18,000 tons an hour in some cases. Inevitably the bottoms of the holds get sudden, regular batterings, which may weaken the structure. Moreover, iron ore, in particular, contains water, which drains out during a voyage, affecting the vessel's stability: it washes around, increasing the swing of the ship.

Lancelot Bedlington, a naval architect, adds another important factor: 'The shore maintenance varies from company to company, and if it is not really up to snuff, this can create problems. If there's any weakness there, bad weather invariably catches it out. Seamen are dying because of it.'

And the solution? 'To a large extent it's a matter of education, more training for people who operate ships – the standards of training vary throughout the world. Overriding all of this, of course, is the financial aspect, the commercial aspect, competition. It's a problem which is not new. Mr Plimsoll was one of the first to come across the similar situation – not ships breaking in two, but the operation of ships in a commercially competitive world where some people maintained, operated and loaded their ships better than others.'

Because the losses were so often of obscure ships in Third World countries, they did not register with the general public, certainly in Britain, until the sinking of the *Derbyshire*, which threw the whole pattern of maritime regulation and investigation into sharp relief. On or about 9 September 1980 (to this day, no one is sure), the 170,000-ton *Derbyshire* sank in the South China Sea, one of the deepest waters in the world, during a trip from Seattle in the USA to Yokohama with a cargo of iron ore. All forty-four people on board – including the wives of two crew members – were drowned in the largest British-registered total loss in maritime history: the ship was four times the size of the *Titanic*. It had been caught up in Typhoon Orchid, but no Mayday calls were sent.

In the absence of an official inquiry the families banded together as the Derbyshire Families Association and began their own investigation – an unthinkable idea with a major air accident which would automatically spark an inquiry. The father of one of the crew was Peter Ridyard, a naval architect. Through his contacts he built up a worrying picture of the *Derbyshire* and her five sister ships, which had been built at the Swan Hunter yard on Tyneside. The evidence seemed to suggest a serious design flaw leading to extensive cracking and structural failure around bulkhead 65, where the bow cargo section joined the space that contained the stern engine and the crew's accommodation. The longitudinal girders did not run through the bulkhead as they had in the original design but had been modified to run up to the bulkhead.

Until 1982 there had been no suspicion of any structural weakness in these ships. That year, says Douglas Faulkner, 'a ship called the *Tyne Bridge*' – of the same class as the *Derbyshire* – 'was in the North Sea on a cold winter's day and had two brittle cracks appearing across the deck at the after-end. This led to people saying, "This is a spot where the structural arrangements are suspect, because there's been some evidence of poor connections between the hold structure and the machinery space." It was more fully investigated then as some other ships were reporting cracks in this area. The families felt they were on to something which might be the real cause for the loss of the ship, that the stern in fact fractured right across the deck and broke away, and that would be why there was no Mayday signal. All would happen very quickly. This theory was supported by theoretical work by a Professor Bishop, who showed that there were some high stresses at such positions. And it all seemed to hang together as a plausible theory.'

In 1986 another sister ship of the *Derbyshire*, the *Kowloon Bridge*, got into difficulties while crossing the Atlantic, with cracks appearing in her structure. The master, Captain Reo, decided to take her into Bantry Bay for investigations and repairs. The survey was duly completed but the weather worsened and he had to leave his moorings. He set off along the south coast of Ireland but lost steering capacity. As the weather conditions worsened the crew was lifted off. (The winchman on the rescue helicopter said it had been the most dangerous rescue he had ever undertaken.) The abandoned ship drifted without her crew until she grounded just south of Cork. Stuck on the rocks she could not be moved by even the most powerful tugs and became a local tourist attraction. Fishermen looted the cabins, divers examined the wreck. Finally she slipped off the rocks and broke in two – probably at bulkhead 65. Within a few months only her funnel was visible.

The first, belated, government report into the loss of the *Derbyshire* concluded that the ship had probably been overcome by the forces of nature, because of the typhoon conditions, and added that the available evidence did not support any firmer findings. One of the experts involved argued that the hatches had been forced off leading to a sudden, catastrophic inrush of water into the hold. His work was rejected by the Commissioner of Wrecks. But the families and the International Transport Federation (ITF) were not convinced by the government report, especially as the Commissioner of Wrecks had refused to allow any consideration of the *Kowloon Bridge*. The ITF financed an expedition to locate and map the wreck of the *Derbyshire*. They commissioned the *Magellan* 725 ROV, a deep-ocean remote-control vehicle designed for high-quality inspection and recovery operations. Using a fibre-optic cable she can transmit video, sonar and data communications. In June 1994, after a month of searching, they found the wreck of the *Derbyshire* on the seabed at a depth of two-and-a-half miles: the debris was scattered over an area of a mile from east to west. The ITF ran out of funds before they could conduct any further investigation.

As a result the British government was shamed into agreeing to set up a new investigation under Lord Doñaldson, with naval expert Professor Douglas Faulkner and Robin Williams as technical assessors. They financed a second, more extensive underwater investigation by the Woods Hole Oceanographic Institute in Massachusetts to find the *Derbyshire* and to make an overall plan of the wreckage.

'Our starting point,' says Faulkner, 'was to say we needed to take a fresh look. And my own particular fresh point was to say, "This is an extraordinary loss of a very big ship, brand new virtually. How could it possibly happen?" And then when you start thinking about it, you realize that the most unusual thing, of course, is the sea itself. I became interested in looking at the type of seas that are generated in typhoons and I found that we were talking about 10 metres or more of water over the deck, because these ships don't move, they just tunnel into the seas. And then you realize that the hatches are quite low strength. It looked like a promising line of investigation.

'We concluded that there may be thirteen possible loss scenarios. They fell broadly into three categories: the structure of the ship, what you might call the fore-end vulnerability to flooding, and then the things like fire, cargo shift, the more operational side.' The investigators judged them all on potential seriousness in a sort of 'risk matrix'. 'And it was because of that we then looked at the hatch-covers more seriously, we had to look at frame 65, which the families, of course, were very keen to prove had been the cause of the weakness. And in that way we progressively reduced the number of scenarios that were in contention.'

If the problem had been the stern coming off, as the ITF survey had suggested, 'Most naval architects would say that wouldn't be the end of the ship, it would be the end of the stern and it would sink very quickly, and the ship would simply be driven by the typhoon until eventually she was overwhelmed, because she had a lot of watertight sub-divisions. She simply wouldn't sink right away. So when you find in 4,000 metres of water depth that the stern and the rest of the ship are only 600 metres apart, that really is almost categorical proof that they were intact at the surface and the separation came later, while they were sinking.'

Instinctively Faulkner 'felt something unusual happened to that ship. And I started myself creating mathematically these cyclonic storms and the waves that would come from them. And those waves I found to my amazement were 25 to 30 metres high, and this is way beyond the sorts of heights that we design ships for . . . When I started looking at the strength of the hatch-covers, I realized they're only designed for 1.7 metres of water. I started regarding that as the most likely cause of the loss. Water can only get in because the ship's side breaks, the deck breaks. Now the hatch-covers occupy 30 per cent of the deck area, and yet their strength is less than one-tenth of that of the rest of the deck. They would fail at four metres and the rest of the deck at something like 50 metres [height of waves].'

Using the full armoury of modern science, they found more corroborative evidence. 'If the ship had broken at frame 65,' says Faulkner, 'the normal expectation would be a fairly clean break of the hull, with straight-line fractures all the way round the deck, down the sides and round the bottom. In the event we found nothing like that. Moreover there is a phenomenon called implosion. We didn't know much about it till we were faced with it. If you take a biscuit tin and submerge it underwater so that eventually the pressure builds up on all the sides of the biscuit tin, it is eventually going to collapse on the weakest side, and in doing so it'll compress the air in the tin until the steel of the tin itself fractures somewhere, because of the enormous strains it's suffering in the distortion. At that point, the compressed air has so much energy it'll just blow open the tin. That is the explosion that follows the initial compression, which we call implosion. And that explains the phenomenon. In the *Derbyshire*, which was double-hulled, you have something like seventy spaces of empty air which can individually collapse and crush, then blow apart. That's exactly what happened with the *Derbyshire*' – an explosion equivalent to 18 tons of TNT.

'If,' continues Faulkner, 'you have implosion taking place at some cross-section, like the wing tanks at the top of the ship bursting and then exploding, they would look mangled, and you'd recognize that as not being a clean break through a ship section, like from brittle fracture. We found structures both forward and aft of frame 65 with implosions, and that necessarily shows that the ship must have been intact at the moment of sinking. That, coupled with the fact that the actual fractures around the frame 65 position were long and wandering and went fore and aft and across the ship and so on, meant that there was absolutely no way she could have broken at the surface. And that disproved the frame 65 scenario absolutely. It's one of the few that you can absolutely rule out.'

Then, by doing a gigantic undersea jigsaw, they pieced together the hatch-covers. They found evidence 'that showed that several hatch-covers were probably burst in by the waves and not just in the act of sinking. So that's supportive evidence for the loss being due to bursting in of the hatch-covers.' One key element was 'a small stores hatch in the forward part of that forepeak deck, which was alleged not to have been properly secured – and certainly the hatch-cover is missing, but there is also a missing windlass. So the sea that actually took off the windlass, which weighed several tons, might easily have swept the hatch-cover off that store.' This would then have filled with water.

Faulkner believes that the sinking occurred at night when the captain wouldn't have been aware of what was happening at the fore-end. 'There's been a history of ships that have had this phenomenon. The *Leros Strength* was another one recently, a very similar type of incident. Really, until you get to the point where the number-one hatch-cover has burst, the captain wouldn't have known, and by then he's lifted up in his seat as the bow starts going down and there's nothing he can do. And it takes perhaps four minutes to get a Mayday signal away – he can't even get a radio message away, because he's got less time than that.'

Faulkner and his colleagues made three principal recommendations. The main one 'is that the hatch-covers are under strength by the old load-line convention they're designed to. To remedy them, we need to increase their strength by two or three times. And I'm happy to note that the bigger classification societies have already taken steps to remedy that with factors between two and three.'

The families accepted that their theories were no longer tenable. Faulkner says, 'I think now they're more concerned to do what they can for ship safety, and particularly safety of big ships, and therefore they will be pressing just as hard as I am for changes in things like the forecastle design, the hatch-covers and so on.'

For his part Mark Dickinson of the ITF concentrates on wider issues. 'The design lessons we can learn from the *Derbyshire* are quite extensive,' he says. As well as the strength of the hatch-covers, 'There's the general point about how these ships are built and their survivability, the cleating mechanisms for the hatches themselves. They should be easy to use for the crew. There is also the question of the deck openings on the forecastle, whether these mushroom-shaped air vents ought to be redesigned because they were clearly swept away, as other openings in the deck were swept away, and therefore there was potential for water to gain access to the spaces forward of number one. There's also this question of protecting the deck and the hatch-covers from breaking seas over the bow. In the case of the *Derbyshire*, and in many bulk carriers built at that time and still being built today, there is just a flush deck. There is nothing to protect the hatch-covers themselves or protect anybody walking on the deck from breaking seas.'

The *Derbyshire* was not the last bulk carrier whose loss caused a major rethink. The latest such example was the *Flare*, a 400-foot bulk carrier with a crew of twenty-five that was sailing empty from Rotterdam to Montreal to pick up a cargo of grain. In early 1998 battling through stormy seas off Newfoundland, the crew became worried about the ship, above all about the ominous cracks in her hull. At 0437 local time on 16 January, the coast-guard at Stephenville on Newfoundland received a garbled Mayday message from a position estimated to be about 75 miles south-west of the island of Saint Pierre and Miquelon. That afternoon a helicopter found the bow section, albeit not in the radioed position. One of the crew, Master Corporal Rob Butler, the flight engineer, describes the scene: they 'started to fly round that and it was probably one of the most eerie things I've ever seen. She was just huge, probably two hundred feet. From the front she looked like a perfectly good ship and then she's just completely torn in half. She was probably 60 feet high and at this time the waves are still rolling halfway up the side of the hull.' To the pilot of the helicopter, Chris Brown, 'She looked like she was a piece of tin, torn apart right at the rear. It was just an incredible sight and the bow was sticking up right out of the water. The back was filling with water and the front was empty. There wasn't much weight because the vessel was empty at the time. You couldn't really believe how this thing had just torn apart. And you can understand how [the crew] had no time at all. She tore apart right where they'd be trying to get off the ship. So if they had had more warning, if they could have just made it up to the bow of the ship – it floated for two days before it finally sank. But they just didn't have time.'

In the hospital the survivors told the rescue team of how the *Flare* had been sailing through rough seas for five days. With no cargo on board they were riding high in the water. 'One of the fellows heard a loud noise in the middle of the night and went up to the deck to check it out. When he looked up he saw the ship breaking apart and the abandon-ship alarm was sounded. Everybody was sleeping, so they were dressed very poorly, boxer shorts, T-shirts, some didn't have any shoes on, and this was January, so it's quite cold. By the time they got up on deck they could see a rescue ship coming to save them. Well, it was the bow – it had broken off and was passing them by the other way. I guess at that point there was no one left on the bridge and the captain ordered the radio fellow to go back up and send out a Mayday. This fellow ran up to the radio room and threw out a message as fast as he could, and that is why we got such a poor position. This guy just wanted to get off that ship.' Because of the list, one of the lifeboats was washed overboard and the other, suspended high above the sea, capsized when it was released. The four survivors said that six had jumped into the icy waters from the stern and swum to the upturned lifeboat, but big waves washed two off and they didn't have the strength to climb back up over the side.

For the Canadian investigators, like Captain Bill McConie, the survivors were not entirely satisfactory witnesses. 'Unfortunately these four were not in the command loop. One was an electrician, one was a seaman, one was a fourth engineer and one was a second cook.' The investigators went round the world of shipping to look for clues to the cause of the disaster but found that no weaknesses had been noted previously in the *Flare* and that she had survived quite comfortably in conditions far more rigorous than those in which she sank. Lloyd's of London, McConie continues, 'with whom we have been dealing, have been very good in this regard. They contacted owners of similar ships of similar age and advised them not only to have a special survey, but to go into even greater depth on the area in which we know the *Flare* broke up, in case there is a weakness in the other ships.'

For his part, McConie believes 'that it was a fracture in the shell-plating and/or the deck-plating, but the origin of this is still to be determined. This is why we're going to have a look at the broken section of the bow. It would be a mirror image, we imagine, of what had happened to the stern section. The stern section is in considerably deeper water than the bow section.'

The investigators' train of thought gives a good insight into modern investigation methods. For Lancelot Bedlington 'the basic question they have to answer first is how the bow separated from the stern and what clues are they looking for'. This they will not know until they have had a look at the submerged part. 'The examination of the submerged vessel will concentrate on the damaged end pieces – in effect, like the end of a broken carrot in the case of brittle fracture. The plate would break very suddenly because of the stresses imposed on it. It can be identified several ways, but primarily because the plate itself is not deformed, there's no deformation of the edges.' The alternative is 'buckling and tearing of the vessel as it came apart underneath. The vessel went down stern first, and the stern unfortunately separated.' Some of the more interesting parts, from the investigators' point of view, may well be buried in the sandy, muddy seabed 'and we may not be able to see all that we would like to see. But until we go down we won't really know.'

Even then, says Bedlington, 'one of our problems will be to decide which damage was likely to have occurred before the vessel sank, and which happened when she hit the bottom. This can be confusing because although hitting the bottom wouldn't have happened very fast, the simple momentum and weight of the vessel would cause plates to buckle. And that buckling can confuse any scenario that you might be able to build up as to the sequence of events.'

For a break-up to occur, says Bedlington, 'the vessel obviously has to be subjected to some considerable strain'. In the case of the *Flare*, 'She was in the North Atlantic in extremely rough weather and she was in a very light-ballasted condition for several days beforehand. She'd been hitting the seas very hard, and because she was so light in the water at the forward end, the bow was pounding and hitting the sea. This would send shock waves shuddering through the ship and the ship would flex, or rip. This constant bending and flexing induced fatigue in what we call the outer fibre and the beam, which is the top layer of the deck, and the bottom, which is the keel. Over the years, this produces fatigue and if there's any sort of discontinuity in the structure, a sudden, concentrated stress build-up occurs that cannot dissipate. The discontinuity could well be structural disintegration or corrosion. Or older vessels are prone to small fatigue cracks, which develop over the years. Very difficult to detect. And discontinuity of that type could produce this high stress concentration that can result in brittle fracture, which is virtually instantaneous across a plate. This is common to all ships, but more so in bulk carriers, simply because of their structural arrangement.'

The likelihood of any brittle fracture spreading depends on the method of construction. As Bedlington explains, 'Many older bulk carriers were built with riveted seams near the deck and just round the bottom turn of the bilge, for the express purpose of preventing or arresting the progress of any fractures which may have occurred. The fracture would not pass across from one riveted plate to another. With a welded structure the stress and the fracture cross through the weld. But if the stress is relieved suddenly, for example as after a sudden pounding, then the brittle fracture could of itself stop.

'The *Flare* was built in 1972 and she's lasted so long that it would lead you to believe that there's nothing inherently wrong with the design. Obviously her maintenance and repair would form part of our investigation. As we look at the vessel with underwater cameras we will have a good idea of her physical condition at the time. As we understand it, the vessel's condition and certificates were up to date, she'd been surveyed recently. At the last special survey, quite a bit of steel was renewed. We have information telling us where and how the new steel was fitted. It was found satisfactory and it's almost two years since that was done.

'However, the welding of new steel to old can create problems. But it's unlikely that an owner would weld good steel to old steel that was clearly not going to last very long. If the surface of the older steel is properly prepared, there's no major problem.'

The investigation could be important. 'As far as I know,' says McConie, 'this is the first occasion that the Transportation Safety Board of Canada has been involved in such an in-depth study of the bulkers, although volumes has been written about earlier losses. Seldom have the flag states or the owners been able to examine these break-ups in detail to establish what went wrong. And we have a golden opportunity in that this one is practically sitting on our own doorstep, and therefore anything that we *can* do we *should* do, to find out what happened – and we must promulgate the information to the shipping industry.'

3
Titanics of the Narrow Seas

With every addition to the active world fleet of ro-ros it has become more and more difficult for designers who are concerned about the position to voice a caution or a protest. Shipbuilders will design to whatever the law allows. Ship-owners' technical staff know where their monthly pay packet comes from and keep quiet.

J.R. Spouge*

The sinking of the *Herald of Free Enterprise*, off Zeebrugge on 6 March 1987, with the loss of thirty-eight crew and 155 passengers remains probably the single most powerful reminder to the British public of the dangers of the sea. For Scandinavians, the loss of another roll-on-roll-off (ro-ro) ferry, the *Estonia*, seven years later, when 852 persons died in the icy waters of the Baltic, is an equally powerful symbol.

The idea of a ferry on which cars, or even trains, could roll on and roll off was not new. During the 1930s a number of train ferries operated across the English Channel but although many such ferries carried cars across the Baltic before 1939 it was only after 1945 that they became commonly used in British waters. The first big British car ferry was the *Princess Victoria*, launched in 1939 for the short crossing between Scotland and Ulster. She was sunk by a mine in May 1940. Her namesake, launched in 1941, was sunk in the terrible gales that swept the British Isles at the end of January 1953. On Saturday 31 January she left Stranraer at 0745. Two and a quarter hours later, unable to turn back in the stormy conditions, she sent out an SOS but foundered before help could arrive.

Only forty-three of the 182 people on board survived, a higher toll than

*'The Technical Investigation of the Sinking of the Ro-ro Ferry *European Gateway*', J. R. Spouge. Paper read to the Royal Institute of Naval Architects, 17 April 1985.

might have been expected because the ship had changed course to try to avoid the worst of the storm and thus the location given on the SOS was incorrect. The master of the *Orchy*, the first vessel on the scene, told the subsequent official inquiry that if rescue ships had reached the ship two hours earlier 'they could have saved quite a lot of lives. Aircraft flying low might have been able to locate the vessel earlier.' As it was the ship was 13 miles south-west of where they thought she was.

Although the victims included an MP, Sir Walter Smiles, and the Northern Island Minister of Finance, Major Maynard Sinclair, there was surprisingly little public reaction to the disaster. This was partly because there had been so many other bigger tragedies in the recent storms: unprecedentedly high tides had wrought havoc all along the east coast of Britain. In addition – and notably unlike the *Herald* disaster – the tragedy did not relate to the experience of most who read about it: few had travelled on such a ship. Also, by June 1953 when the report on the accident came out, the country was concentrating on the coronation of the young Queen Elizabeth II and the first British ascent of Mount Everest.

Yet, significantly, the report had pointed to the design flaws that produced other disasters thirty-five years later. The stern gates had been stove in by a heavy sea so that the car deck had been flooded, and the ship had started to list to starboard. One witness, a consulting engineer, told the inquiry that the design was unsafe because the arrangement for staying the doors was too weak and, above all, because the doors were vertical: 'If the staying pins were sheared and the sliding bolts were bent there was nothing at all to keep the doors in position. . . The pressure to shear these doors would be less than that necessary to fracture or buckle the plates of these doors.' The report concluded that the scuppers on the car deck, which may well have been blocked by paint, were too small to clear the mass of accumulated water – and that the stern gates had not been strong enough.

The ship's owners, the British Transport Commission, should have been alerted by two earlier incidents to the dangers presented by stern doors. In the worst, in November 1951, the stern doors broke open while the *Princess Victoria* was sailing stern first into Larne harbour in gale-force winds – a condition likely to be repeated in the notoriously choppy waters of the Irish Channel. The master wrote to his superiors asking for bigger scuppers to be fitted to help drain the water. But the management was not local – another factor criticized by the inquiry – and there was no one in the organization 'whose sole duty it was to look after the well-being of the structure of the ships'. But, in an uncanny foretaste of what happened with the *Herald of Free Enterprise*, the management merely repaired the doors, dismissing the reports with jokes about inconvenience to 'ladies with fancy shoes and nylon stockings' of water slopping around the car deck and the protest letters as 'so much waste paper'. Its representatives even told the inquiry that 'Men have different characters. Some delight in making a fuss about everything'.

One of the most fundamental regulations established following the *Titanic* disaster was supposed to ensure that the hull of every sea-going ship was divided into watertight compartments. Yet such ships, and their many successors, were designed to enable vehicles to roll on at one end and roll off at the other. To be economic, their car decks had to be open and thus free from any obstruction. Once water got into the car deck there were no bulkheads to stop it spreading through the 'free-surface effect' and, within a few minutes, destabilizing the ship.

Richard Johnson of the National Transportation Safety Board (NTSB) explains: 'The free-surface effect means that water sloshes back and forth. If you've ever carried a tray of water you'll have seen that the water flips from one side to another. When you have bulkheads to interrupt the movement of water, you can reduce the effect of water in a compartment.' But 'ro-ro' ferries are one big open compartment.

The *Princess Victoria* inquiry also revealed that the design of the life jackets was defective, liaison between the shore wireless station and the coastguard was imperfect and, more importantly, that rescue arrangements – particularly tugs – were inadequate.

The first vessel to be built that absorbed all the recommendations made after the *Princess Victoria* tragedy was the *Maid of Kent*, launched in 1959 for the increasingly important route from Dover to Calais. She had a hydraulically operated stern door designed to be completely watertight. It formed part of the hull, and was hinged horizontally so that it could be raised out of the way during loading. This design was also followed on the *Free Enterprise* class of ro-ro ferries ordered by Townsend Thoresen, the pioneers of such ships.

The growth of mass car-borne tourism, most of it on the short-haul cross-Channel routes, ensured that ro-ro ferries became a routine form of transport for millions of holidaymakers, carrying over twenty million passengers across the English Channel every year. But the ships remained inherently dangerous: between 1978 and 1988 over 5,300 passengers were killed in ferry accidents the world over, meaning that ferry travel was ten times as dangerous as air travel – if only because so inherently unsafe a design would never have been accepted by the aviation authorities. For British travellers the dangers were graphically illustrated in December 1982, when the ro-ro ferry *European Gateway* was holed in the side after a collision with a freighter. Heeling over quickly after 'a wall of water hit the engine room', six aboard were drowned.

By then naval architects were only too aware of the dangers and of their helplessness in the face of the commercial pressures involved, which ensured that there was no adequate compartmentalization within the car deck. As R. A. Cahill wrote, 'These ships are inherently unseaworthy.'*

Nevertheless the dangers had become a public scandal only after the sinking of the *Herald of Free Enterprise* on 6 March 1987. The worst peacetime calamity to affect a British-registered ship since the *Titanic* revealed not only the basic flaw in the design of all such vessels but also appallingly inadequate management.

The ferry was on a regular service to Dover from the Belgian port of Zeebrugge. On board were a crew of eighty and 500 passengers, many of whom were returning from a day-trip to Belgium sponsored by the *Sun* newspaper. The weather was good, the sea calm. About a mile out to sea the *Herald of Free Enterprise* lurched to port while swinging to starboard, before progressively tilting over further and further as passengers and furniture slid and smashed across the deck, hitting the glass windows on the port side. Within little more than a minute she had capsized and settled on her beam ends facing the way she had come. Water began to flood into all the decks, and two-thirds of the ship was soon submerged.

It quickly became clear quickly that the bow doors had still been open when the *Herald* left Zeebrugge, allowing thousands of gallons of sea-water to pour into the car deck. At first the water caused only a slight list to port but this increased until she tilted over at a right angle. The principal investigator into the disaster was Captain Brian Vale. He was a senior inspector in the Ship Survey Service, which at the time investigated accidents. He pieced together the exact course of the disaster: 'Everything went normally until the vessel was past the outer wall. Shortly after that the steward who

Disasters at Sea R.A. Cahill, Fairplay Publications, London, 1990.

looked after the drivers' accommodation in the deck below the car deck saw water coming down the stairway. He rang the purser's office, thinking it was probably a plumbing problem, and a call was put out from the purser's office for the carpenter to investigate.

'On the bridge, the people who had been to harbour stations were dispersing to their watch-keeping stations. There was the master, two quartermasters and the second officer, Paul Mortar, and the chief officer. As they got clear of the [harbour] entrance the master allowed both the officers to go down and get their meal. He would stay on watch until one of them came back to relieve him. They had no sooner got down to the officers' mess than the vessel started to take a list and it was such that both of them realized that it was something serious, not just a roll due to a course alteration. They both dashed back to the bridge. At practically the same time, a fire alarm sounded on the bridge, one of the quartermasters went to the board and found it was from one of the port stairways down aft. Before he had time to cancel it and ask one of the engineers to investigate, the ship started to go over.

'Passing the outer wall the vessel was going at about nine or ten knots. The master increased the speed and shortly after he put the engines ahead more. Then the list increased suddenly. Just as this happened the quartermaster on the wheel said that he had the wheel hard a-port, and the vessel was going to starboard, which, of course, was highly unusual in the weather conditions, which were good. Almost immediately the vessel continued right over, and at the same time turned sharply to starboard until she finally took an almost 180-degree turn and ended up on her port side in shallow water, about three-quarters of a mile from the entrance.

'The routine was for the assistant bosun to close the doors when harbour stations were called or, if someone else had already done that, to check that the doors were closed properly. It was the job of the loading officer on G deck to check that the doors were secure. On this occasion it was the chief officer who finished off the loading, and his harbour station was on the bridge, assisting the master as the ship backed out and turned. According to one set of instructions, he should have seen that the doors were closed, and according to another he should have been on the bridge with the master. This really put him in a bizarre situation in that he was required to be in two places at once. In the past it had been accepted that the loading officer saw the assistant bosun at the controls, ready to close the doors, and then went to the bridge. This had been accepted as being okay for seeing that the doors were secure. On this occasion, the chief officer went to the bridge without making certain that the assistant bosun was at the controls. If the assistant bosun has any trouble closing the doors, he's got a telephone to the bridge, so it is assumed that unless he calls, they've been closed properly. So the chief officer went to the bridge and there was no one on the controls. This had come about because this was what they called a maintenance voyage. The chief officer was badly injured, but was certain that he'd seen somebody approaching the position where the controls are and that he assumed it was the assistant bosun – which is why he felt free to go up to the bridge.

'Normally the assistant bosun assists the rest of the crew in loading the car deck, directing vehicles and putting chains on wagons or whatever's necessary, and then he goes to his harbour station, which is closing the doors. But on a maintenance voyage he supervises the rest of the crew who are doing normal painting, scraping, cleaning round the ship. He made a last round to see that the jobs that were allocated had been done, and when he got back to the car deck where the bosun was on loading duties, he spoke to the bosun, who told him to knock off until harbour stations. So he was quite within his rights to go to his cabin. There he made himself a cup of tea. He sat on his bunk reading, and nodded off. The first he knew was when the vessel went over. So that was the primary cause.'

Mark Stanley, the assistant bosun, 'had the reputation of being one of the best in the business, very conscientious. When he didn't close the doors, he always checked that they had been properly closed by whoever else had done them.' With Vale he was 'completely open, made no bones about what he'd done, and I believed everything that he told me'.

The rescue services arrived within a quarter of an hour but this was already too late for many of those trapped on board; 193 perished in a chaos of flying glass and other debris. It was nothing short of a miracle that four-fifths of those on board survived. Fortunately, most of the passengers had immediately made for the restaurants and duty-free shops, both of which were on the upper decks. It also helped that the ferry settled on a sandbank as she turned over. People on the lower decks below the saloons stood little chance of rescue: the cross-passages tilted and became vertical tunnels and it was clearly impossible to climb them.

The survival rate was also helped by the efficiency of the rescue services and the heroism of the crew. As Vale explains: 'The crew's mess room was on the starboard side, so that when she went over to port they were going for their evening meal after sailing. Quite a number were able to get out on to the starboard side of the ship and they made their way along the side, first of all to the bridge. Led by the bosun, Mr Terry Ayling, they first got the people out of the bridge, the master, the mate, quartermaster and the second officer. The master and mate were pretty badly injured, and all they could do was lay them on the side of the vessel – they could take no leading role in the rescue operations. But Mr Ayling took charge and, urging the rest of the crew along, started smashing the windows in the accommodation. He was able to do this because of his knowledge of the lifeboats, which contained axes, ropes, torches and things like that. The assistant bosun was involved in this too, and he cut his arms pretty badly scooping the glass out of the windows when they were smashed. He also went down a rope and entered the accommodation, which was pretty brave because it was pitch black, cold, no lights. Quite a large number of the survivors were got out by the crew. They were at it for something like two hours, they were cold, wet, exhausted, as you can imagine, as well as traumatized by the event. And, of course, within a short time the vessel was surrounded by all kinds of other vessels, tugs, a dredger that had originally seen her came out, pilot boats. There were helicopters, more and more vessels came, divers, naval vessels, you name it. It was an enormous search and rescue operation.'

Most of the crew were applauded, as were some passengers like Andrew Parker who made himself into a human bridge, but not, unfortunately, Terry Ayling, the bosun. While in the witness box at the inquiry he had said something to the effect that 'It was never part of my job to close the doors'. Unfortunately, says Vale, 'This gave a very bad impression to the court, in the sense that it was taken to mean that it's a sort of union demarcation thing – "I wouldn't do that job." In effect what he meant was that at harbour stations everybody has their own job and you go and do your own job, otherwise if you start doing your own thing you descend into chaos.'

The crucial factor in the disaster was that 'there was no positive reporting system'. This particularly shocked Captain Vale, used to the formality normal in orthodox ship operation. 'Over the years – and, of course, this vessel had been running for seven on a very frequent service – undoubtedly complacency had come into it, and the system laid down in the instructions was that if the master did not receive a report from any of the heads of department that something was wrong at sailing time, then he would assume that everything was all right. This was quite wrong; things should be the other way round. People should carry out whatever their duty is and then report to the master that it was done, in this case that the doors had been closed. This was the basic fault of the whole system' – even though it had been endorsed by all the five masters who had sailed the *Herald*.

But, of course, they were not in charge. The executives in the firm's head office were far more responsible. After interviewing the responsible shore-based managers, 'The main feature that came out of it,' says Vale, 'was that nobody was designated as responsible for general safety in operational procedures as such. In what I might call an ordinary shipping company, as distinct from a ferry company, there would be the marine superintendent in charge of all these things, and the masters would report to him and so on. In the Townsend Thoresen ferry set-up, one of the five masters was designated as the senior master, and he was supposed to be acting, rather vaguely I feel, as the equivalent of a marine superintendent. I don't think he had the clout or the authority that a marine superintendent should have had.'

At the time the company was expanding rapidly 'with the new types of ferries and the excellent service they were giving. And I don't think they actually sat down and looked at the structure of the company. Things had just grown up instead of being properly structured with responsibilities defined directly. Safety, and the operation of the ships, wasn't the direct responsibility of any one person.' This was directly against the guidelines issued by the Department of Transport.

It didn't help that 'those of the head-office managers who had been to sea were engineers and more concerned with the hardware of ship management – building, repairs, maintaining and so on, not what you might call the software, the operation. Their fault lay in not listening to their highly competent senior masters.' That's putting it mildly. The court was naturally annoyed by the tone of some of the management's memos in response to the request for indicator lights: 'One of the replies asked if they needed a light to tell them that the assistant bosun is awake and sober.'

Investigators carried out extensive tests, which showed how free-surface water rolling around the car deck could quickly destabilize a ship. Further tests showed that the bow of the *Herald* had been loaded with ballast to lower her by between two and three feet to enable her to use Zeebrugge. Moreover, the ship was travelling at 17.5 knots – if she had been going a knot slower she would not have sunk. This was down to commercial pressure for a quick turn-round. The tests also demonstrated the gruesome fact that this type of boat reaches maximum stability when she is upside down.

The tragedy produced results in the form of improved reporting systems, safety procedures, and video cameras for the bow doors so that they could be seen from the bridge. By contrast, proposals for the introduction of bulkheads on the car deck remain largely a dead letter even though the loss of revenue, and the increased inconvenience, would be less serious than is claimed by the operators. The disaster also produced a shake-up in the way the British government organized its marine investigations. In the past, says John Lang, of the Marine Accidents Investigations Branch, they were 'conducted by the same surveyors [like Vale] or organization as those who made the regulations and enforced them. That continued until the *Herald of Free Enterprise* sank. At the subsequent inquiry it became clear that the Department of Transport was both the regulatory authority and also the body that directly employed the investigators. Hence the establishment of the independent Marine Accident Association in 1989.'

Vale's conclusions were optimistic. 'The court of formal investigation made recommendations for the short-term, medium-term and long-term, and certainly the short-term requirements were carried out within twelve months – indicator lights, closed-circuit television, operations manuals. All this, with proper instructions and reporting procedures, made this type of accident . . . one never says impossible when you're talking about safety, but virtually, and from the operations point of view, certainly ferries are very safe now.' Well, up to a point.

The most tragic example of the results of inherent flaws in the design of ro-ro ferries came with the 21,000-ton *Estonia*. She sank in the early hours of 27 September 1994, during a bad storm while she was on her regular westward crossing from Tallinn, the capital of Estonia, to Stockholm. Only 137 people survived out of the 989 aboard. It was the worst ever peacetime loss to a passenger ship in Western Europe.

The official story of the disaster, contained in a report by a joint commission representing the Swedish, Estonian and Finnish governments, has been challenged by an independent report commissioned by the German builders of the *Estonia*. The contradictory versions – together with efforts, above all by the Swedish government, to prevent further investigation – have led to the emergence of a host of conspiracy theories.

The *Estonia* was no ordinary ferry but a symbol of the opening up to the West of the former Soviet satellites in the Baltic. She provided the most important direct route for passengers and lorries from the newly independent Baltic states to Western Europe. As a result she unwittingly became a well-known channel for smuggling drugs and illegal immigrants from the former Soviet Union to Western Europe.

Rumours surrounding the fate of the *Estonia* abound. Possibly the most exotic is that the Russian–Estonian Mafia had placed a limpet mine on the starboard bilge tank, designed to cripple the ship as a warning that the shipping company should pay protection money. Unfortunately the mine went off at the wrong time. The Mafia hadn't realized what a terrible state the ship was in and how vulnerable it was to the smallest explosion. It was also said that two closely guarded military trucks were on board, which had been loaded under close military protection. Did they – as the theory goes – contain military-quality cobalt from somewhere in the former Soviet Union?

The course of the disaster was that at 0040 the crew reported a loud bang from the bow of the ship. Thirty-five minutes later, water was seen on the ship's TV monitor seeping into the car deck from openings along the vertical side of the forward ramp. Five minutes later the code word for the emergency alert to the crew ('Mr Skylight') was broadcast over the ship's public-address system. A few minutes later the master, Aavo Andressen, sent a Mayday: 'We now have bad problem. Bad list.' That was the last word from the ship and within twenty minutes all radar contact had been lost. In a storm that whipped up waves of thirty feet the *Estonia* had capsized to almost 90 degrees starboard – she was virtually on her side – about twenty miles south of the coast of Finland.

That anyone on board survived was miraculous since most of the passengers were asleep in their cabins when the ship started to sink and the temperature of the water was only 8°C, giving a survival time of about an hour. Not surprisingly, most survivors were suffering from hypothermia while eighty-five people died awaiting rescue.

The best account of the accident comes from a sailor. Silva Linde was on his routine watch round. At a little before one o'clock he came to the car deck and went to the ramp. He had difficulty in keeping his balance in the rough seas. While he was standing a few metres from the ramp he heard a loud, metallic bang, which he reported to the bridge. He was asked by the mate to stay on the car deck. He waited there for a few minutes but did not hear anything and continued his round, ending on the bridge without hearing any other suspicious sound. But within a few minutes, says Tuomo Karppinen, a leading member of the official commission of inquiry, 'someone was calling to the bridge that there were metallic noises from the bow area, from the ramp or from the visor (a metal hood rather similar to those worn by medieval knights), and Linde was then sent down to check what caused these loud noises. He was not able to wake up or contact the bosun – he perhaps did not have his walkie-talkie on him. The mate promised that he would contact the bosun and Linde went downwards. He did not go the shortest way, but soon he came to the information kiosk to ask for the fire doors to the car deck to be opened. He was waiting there because the girl in the information kiosk was changing money for a passenger who had been playing at the casino. During that time the ship started rolling, all the money was thrown on the floor and Linde asked for the doors to the car deck to be opened again. He started running down towards the foredeck and when he got there many passengers were coming up the stairs and some were crying that there was water on the first deck. Linde was not able to go further down because of the crowd of escaping passengers and he turned and ran to the seventh deck. From there he took his walkie-talkie and informed the bridge that there was water on the first deck.' No one from the bridge survived so all we know is that they slowed the ferry down.

The key to the disaster lay in the design, maintenance and the flaws in the front of the *Estonia*. The car deck had a ramp hinged at the bottom, which was covered by the visor. The ship was of similar design to an earlier ferry of the same type, the *Diana 2*, but had a longer ramp than her predecessor. The lengthening involved the construction of a 'ramp house' that covered the tip of the ramp, which would otherwise have stuck up above the deck of the ship. The visor, which weighed around 55 tons, was hinged at the top on the foredeck, and secured by hydraulic and manual locks on each side and another hydraulically operated lock on the centre-line at the bottom, known as an 'Atlantic' lock.

Within a day of the accident, the Swedish government had appointed an accident investigation commission, with members from Finland and Estonia as well as from Sweden. The commission immediately announced that the vessel had sunk because the bow visor had been forced open after the inadequate locking system had failed. The final report looked impressive with charts, graphs and computer-generated graphics. It stated that the locks on the visor had been well maintained but had failed because the mechanism had been under-designed and poorly built.

Following this mechanical failure the visor was cracked open by the force of the waves. It was left hanging from its two hydraulic lifting cylinders, allowing it to smash into the inner doors, which doubled as the vessel's loading ramp. Finally, the bow broke off, water flooded into the car deck, leading to loss of stability, and the vessel capsized less than twenty minutes after the damage had been sustained. Also, the basic design parameters of the bow door had been miscalculated so that it was of unsuitable construction.

This was clearly not the first time such problems had been encountered: the commission learned of more than ten incidents on the ship in which visor lockings had broken. In some instances, the visor had opened and in all the opening of the visor had been observed on the bridge. Quick action was taken: the ship was slowed down, turned and was able to sail to sheltered waters then return to harbour. In 1985, just after the *Mariella* had started to ply between Helsinki and Stockholm, all her lockings broke and, as Karppinen says, 'The visor beams were almost completely broken so that the visor opened but it did not fall down. The crew on the bridge saw what happened then slowed down and the ship sailed to port. Later an inspection of the *Estonia*'s sister vessel, the *Diana 2*, revealed that all the lockings on the starboard side had been ripped off.' Even after that not all the locking mechanisms were reinforced, and the damage to the *Diana 2* was dismissed because she was so old – the Swedish Maritime Administration claims that it never received a report on the incident.

The announcement that the disaster was due to a design fault infuriated Meyer Werft, the well respected German firm that had built the *Estonia*, and they set in train their own investigation, which included metallurgists and naval engineers. They soon uncovered a whole host of anomalies, as well as gaps in the Swedish investigation which hadn't even bothered to interview the survivors. The Germans did – and reached the conclusion that the commission's report was a politically inspired whitewash. 'The commission was chaired by Estonia,' says Captain Werner Hummel, one of the German investigators. 'The first chairman was Andi Meister, the then transport minister of Estonia, and in this capacity the chairman of the supervisory board of Esline and of Esco [the *Estonia*'s owning and operating companies] and his number two was the head of the nautical department and safety adviser of Esline, so these guys were investigating against themselves. For this reason, of course, they were looking for a cause far away from Estonia, Finland, Sweden – and that left Meyer Werft in Germany.'

The first point made by the German investigator's report was that the weather at the time of the disaster was not nearly as bad as the commission had made out. However, Karppinen says, 'There are good reasons to believe that during the accident night the *Estonia* encountered the worst-ever wave conditions and those conditions broke the visor lockings'. But the waves measured only four metres, half the size of the biggest ever recorded, and, as he admits, 'Such conditions are encountered in the northern Baltic and develop between Helsinki and Stockholm five times every year on the average'.

The next bone of contention came with the absence of collision bulkheads. Karppinen agrees that 'The ramp was too close to the bow, compared to the service regulations. It should have been a couple of metres further back. On some vessels built at about the same time as the *Estonia*, the Finnish Maritime Administration required that the partial collision bulkhead should be built at the proper place required by the SOLAS regulations (see p. 15), but in the case of the *Estonia* and *Diana 2*, this type of partial collision bulkhead was not built.' The construction was too weak but nothing was done because once a ship has been inspected she is considered safe. Even though the loadings may have increased, she is 'grandfathered' – exempted from new regulations.

Because permission had initially been given for the *Estonia* to operate only within twenty miles of the coast, the absence of bulkheads did not seem critical; but in 1992, thirteen years after she was built, she transferred to the Estonian flag* and changed her route, plying in the open Baltic Sea from Tallinn to Stockholm, and not only across the narrow Gulf of Bothnia to Helsinki. Bureau Véritas, the French classification society responsible for certifying that the ship was safe, had either not been told of the change of use, with all the increased exposure to bad weather it involved, or had let the ship be grandfathered. In any case the society had a conflict of interest in that it was acting both for the regulators and the owners.

The next suspicious point concerned the visor, now lying upside down on the quayside in Hanko in Finland, existing proof that the official report

*In fact, to satisfy the European Bank for Reconstruction and Development, which was lending the Estonians the money to buy the ship, it was registered in Cyprus.

was not credible. In the words of a well-respected naval architect, Nigel Ling,*

> The inside of the visor has the appearance of a ballast tank. The
> bottom is corroded – with 'tide marks' showing that water had
> repeatedly got into the space between the ramp and the visor. There
> were witnesses prepared to testify that 'when the vessel was entering
> sheltered waters, water could be seen streaming out of the visor
> joint' – a point confirmed by the ship's inspector. In other words,
> 'The visor was, in effect, a free-flooding compartment'.

The skipper of a pilot boat had earlier sent a written warning that water was habitually streaming out of the visor.

Worse, the German inquiry found that the hinges of the visor were worn, their strength at the time of the accident 'little more than 15 per cent of the original construction'. The stern post on which the visor rested had fatigue cracks covered with paint. Revealingly, there were footprints in the hydraulic oil inside the visor showing that the Atlantic lock could no longer be operated hydraulically '– hence all the oil inside the visor – but was hammered open and shut'. The state of the Atlantic lock is illuminated by the extraordinary story, recounted by Ling, that one Swedish seaman 'had carried out repairs to the Atlantic lock on one, possibly two occasions in a manner that can best be described as imaginative. The bosun was aware of this and subsequently, on 12 June 1996, when the two were serving together on the *Fernia*, the bosun shot his colleague dead.' For once Ling departs from his normal severe, technical prose style to comment, '*Estonia* had claimed another victim. Just what events had been taking place on the ship to sufficiently motivate one man to take the life of another?'

As a result of the deplorable state of the bow, the visor, the ramp, their various hinges and locking mechanisms, Ling concludes that 'the vessel proceeded to sea with the port side of the ramp secured by nothing more than one partly engaged hydraulic lock. The second line of defence, the ramp, was no more secure than the first line of defence, the visor – while the third line of defence, the collision bulkhead extension, had never existed.' The Germans also pointed to an amateur video of the ship, which showed the state of the visor's hinges, evidence dismissed by the commission on technical grounds.

*In *Naval Architect* April 1998, a most valuable article.

The German theory supported the idea that the fundamental problem was that the ship was being employed in seas more dangerous than those for which she had been designed, that the strains this involved produced weaknesses in the ramp and visor mechanism, which had received only botched repairs, and that, in general, the ship was poorly maintained. This was a generally accepted fact. When the ship was docked for her annual inspection in 1993 the crew was asked what repairs should be carried out. According to persistent rumours, the sailors involved asked for both the ramp and visor lockings to be reinforced, and this item was subsequently included in the quotation to the repair yard. But then the ship was sold, the work pattern changed, and nothing was done. Even Karppinen admits that the rubber seals on the visor needed renewing. But, he says, 'This is not important: the visor is designed to rest on steel pads and not on the rubber packing. This is just there to seal the visor, to prevent water coming in' – though he acknowledges that a little water could thus have got into the car deck.

The German explanation, confirmed by an independent report commissioned by the ITF, supposes that the first damage started at the Atlantic lock and thus in the lower part of the hull, which frightened the passengers in the cabins below the car deck into coming up on to deck (and thus ensuring that they stood some chance of being saved). The ship 'became open to the sea' and the master tried to right the subsequent list to starboard while desperate efforts were made to haul the ramp and visor back into place. Any hope of compensating the list had gone because the ship was often loaded eccentrically and the side tanks were used to compensate for the resulting lopsidedness. Karppinen admits, 'When the ship was loaded in Tallinn so much cargo, trucks and cars were taken on the starboard side, that to balance for the list caused by the cargo, the port-side tank was almost full. That was partly due to cargo, but also partly because the centre of gravity of the *Estonia* was a little on the starboard side.'

Finally, there had been a training inspection of the ship the very afternoon before she sailed but the senior Swedish inspector did not notice anything wrong that was relevant to the way in which the ship sank. Yet, as witnesses testified, the ramp had been leaking and the crew had put rags, mattresses and blankets into the gaps to stop water entering the car deck.

There were many other suspicious points. When the wreck was located on the seabed the 57-ton curved steel bow visor was found a mile west of the wreck. Yet, according to the inquiry, it should have been to the east, since it was supposed to have come off before the ship was sunk – further support to the German theory that the weakness was general and had not started with the inadequate design of the visor. Moreover, the Atlantic lock, a vital piece of evidence, was recovered but thrown back into the sea because, allegedly, it was too heavy to be transported by helicopter back to land!

Werner Hummel sums up the sequence of events leading to the sinking of what he describes flatly as an 'unseaworthy ship'. 'The visor was open to the outside due to missing rubber packings, while the inside of the visor quickly filled up to the outside level as soon as the bow wave rose; so the visor was filled, say, from 0030 onwards with some 120 to 130 tons of water, moving water, trying to follow the abrupt movement of the vessel pitching in head-on seas. Also, the bow ramp was, with the [tacit approval] of the technical managers, untied for several months because the port outer hinge was broken. The ramp was difficult to close and difficult to open. The crew had put that on the repair list frequently but repairs were postponed by the technical managers to the next planned yard stay, which was in January '95, so the crew had to help in the best terms possible by putting mattresses, blankets and rags in this open part of the bow ramp, which was in the port lower corner. The whole bow ramp was severely misaligned so it did not close, not only at the port lower corner but also at the port upper corner, and the misalignment was so extensive that the locking bolts didn't fit any more at the port side, only at the starboard side.'

Once the vessel 'was exposed fully to the open swell and sea coming from different directions in the middle of the Baltic, the water was rising in the visor, and the blankets, rags and mattresses, which probably could just prevent the worst when the visor was filled up to the third stringer level [horizontal rib], could not withstand this water column of five or six metres so water started to stream on to the car deck. At about quarter to one, when the weather was severely setting in, we assume one of the unsecured trucks moved forward, squeezing some of the cars against the bow ramp. The only partly secured bow ramp fell into the visor, leaning on the flaps, and water poured in increasing quantities on to the car deck.

'The watchman came down at ten to one and told the bridge. Those on the bridge had only one option, to go in to the shelter of the island of Hiiumaa. The Finnish coast was deadly to them, all rocks and small, narrow entries, so they turned the boat to port and took the sea directly from forward which meant, of course, a change of some 60 degrees to port, approximately, and then they reduced the speed by reducing the pitch of the two propellers. This was felt very clearly by everybody on board and was testified to by a large number of surviving passengers, even crew. So the vessel, instead of setting in very quickly and properly, very hard, pitching, suddenly changed to make soft movements.

'A couple of minutes later, at exactly one o'clock, the vessel was shaken first by one and then by another shock and a little bit later, probably a minute or so, heeled to about 50 or 60 degrees starboard and came back to probably 10 degrees. From there on she listed or heeled slowly to starboard until, within the next thirty minutes, she was on her side and lost.'

The final German conclusion, again backed by the ITF report, was that there was nothing inherently wrong with the design but that the bow mechanism had been bent in a previous collision. Moreover, it had been tampered with.

The mysteries remain. Why was the bow door found a whole mile away? Did this mean that the boat had changed direction? Did the water enter because of damage to the hull below the waterline, as some suggested, and not through the bow doors? Why was the ship so slow to call for help?

Even Karppinen admits that the case of the *Estonia* showed that 'There had been a clear difference between the formal definition of seaworthy and the technical definition of seaworthy'. Since the accident, 'The strength of locking has been increased, watertight doors have been installed and incident-reporting systems are being developed and applied. In many ways the mistakes which were made before the *Estonia* accident are now being corrected, and on the basis of the present state of safety of ro-ro passenger ferries an accident like *Estonia* should not be possible.'

For his part, Mikal Oun, a member of a survivors' group, the Neptuners, remains sceptical of the inquiry's report: 'The first thing was that the prime minister said that everything should be done to recover the wreck. And then the government started to work to find out if it was possible and how to do it and if it was morally correct to do that. Then a council was set up with some priests and other people, giving advice to the government on how to deal with all the dead bodies that were left in the ship. This council suggested that they should not recover the ship and they should leave her in the sea.' Yet, he says, 'When they were investigating if it was possible to recover the wreck, they were filming inside it – my personal reaction is that if you can film the dead bodies in the wreck then you can recover them too. But this council gave the advice to the government that they should not recover anything, and that to prevent grave plunderers they should make a cover over the ship.' Oun's group still wants the bodies recovered. He thinks that the government decided not to do so because 'they could not bring up everybody, so they decided to leave the ship in the sea'. They did not want to disappoint relatives of those whose bodies could not be recovered. This surprise decision led to protests, which increased when the government then decided that the next stop would be to bury the wreck to avoid grave plundering. Oun is not alone in finding that 'It's a strange way to do it. If we can now recover the dead bodies then why not? Then there would be no need to cover the wreck to avoid grave plunderers.'

As it is, the answer to all the questions posed by the Germans and the survivors which might help prevent future disasters, lies in the wreck, an untouchable national monument, due to be buried with sand. 'Is this,' asks Nigel Ling, 'the ultimate cover-up?' But let the final word go to the ITF, which issued its own report much on the lines of the German one. 'Throughout the report,' says Mark Dickinson of the ITF, 'they're trying to make sure certainly that nobody in Sweden, Finland and Estonia takes any of the blame. Our report highlights a reluctance to criticize any of the authorities involved in the investigation. I think that's a polite way of saying this is a stitch-up.'

But what are the authorities trying to hide? Perhaps they are anxious not to reveal the inadequacies of the Estonian inspection and certification system, and Sweden's acquiescence in this. But unless the three governments reverse their policy of cover-up, far more sinister explanations will continue to flourish.

4
The Maritime Underworld

Gross negligence, inefficiency, corruption and other malpractices.
Report on the loss of the ferry *Bukoba*.

In terms of sheer loss of life, the most regular disasters occur on over-crowded ferries run, often in narrow, crowded waters of underdeveloped countries whose governments are usually corrupt, almost invariably ineffi-cient. The loss of life is the greater because ferries are the major form of travel for most inhabitants of many such countries.

The figures tell a grim story. In the years between 1963 and 1996 there were thirty-two such disasters and over a hundred people died in each. Eighteen – including most of those involving the heaviest death tolls – took place in only three countries, all poor, all heavily reliant on ferry transport: in Bangladesh – scene of six disasters – many people live clustered round rivers; Indonesia, where five happened, and the Philippines, which holds the record with seven, are archipelagos whose population is scattered over hun-dreds of islands.

But the death toll is not confined to countries over-reliant on water trans-port. On New Year's Day 1989 an overcrowded Guatemalan ferry sank in rough seas with the loss of 'at least' eighty-three lives (typically, in such stories, no one knows the exact size of the passenger list) while she was being towed to port after developing engine trouble. The latest such tragedy occurred on Africa's largest lake, Victoria, when the Belgian-built 800-ton *Bukoba* sank on 21 May 1996 with the loss of an estimated 870 persons. The official figure of 633 passengers, which was probably exceeded by over 300, was well over her legal limit of 411.

Within a few minutes of being hit by high waves the ferry capsized. There had been no time to send a distress signal and the first rescue efforts were made by local fishermen. Tragically, they had to wait several hours for cutting equipment to be brought to the scene and by the time they had gained access to the upturned hull everyone in it was dead – although many had survived for several hours in a series of air pockets. Nevertheless, they had known they were doomed: several had written little notes with their names on them. The divers who eventually recovered the bodies found that many passengers had linked arms in solidarity moments before death and could not be separated. They found the body of a businessman who had been entombed alive for a full two days inside the upturned hull. He had written a last despairing note in Swahili, which he had carefully stowed in his clothes: 'We sealed the doors with bedsheets and the only thing we need is oxygen. We lived until the 23rd but now we are finished.' The ensuing inquiry blamed Tanzania's railway corporation for operating an unstable vessel. 'TRC Marine Operations,' it stated in a conclusion that could be applied to many similar organizations, 'were characterized by gross negligence, inefficiency, corruption and other malpractices.'

In many of the disasters the captain was not at fault: as with the *Princess Victoria* and the *Herald of Free Enterprise*, those who had to sail the vessel knew what was wrong. So it was in January 1970, when 338 people were drowned in the wreck of the relatively tiny 250-ton *Gurita* ferry off the coast of Weh, the northernmost island in the Indonesian archipelago. It was later alleged that the captain had initially refused to leave port after he had found that the ordinary cement being used to plug a leak in the vessel had not fully dried. He sailed only after being threatened with dismissal.

More typical of the combination of bad weather and hysterical chaos that surrounds many such disasters was the loss in 1993 of the thirty-nine-year-old Haitian motor ferry *Neptune*. The ship was grossly overcrowded: it was licensed to carry 250 passengers and officially 'only' 820 people were aboard, but unofficial estimates put the figure at around 2,000. The ship capsized during a sudden squall early in the morning off western Haiti after hundreds of passengers had rushed from one side of the ferry to the other to try to shelter under tarpaulins from the torrential rain. The mass movement destabilized the ship. According to officials, the ship had neither life jackets, rafts, nor even a radio. There were only 285 survivors, 'many of whom,' wrote one investigator, 'had clung to floating animal carcasses or buoyant bags of charcoal for up to thirty-one hours before reaching shore'.

But the worst such accidents have occurred in the Philippines among its seven thousand islands, only nine hundred of which are inhabited. They are connected by ferries, which constitute the main transport links binding the country together. The Filipino fleet includes about a hundred sizeable passenger-cargo ships of over a hundred tons, around two hundred small ferries and thousands of small barges and ships on short runs. The ferries are cheap and transport over eleven million passengers every year but they are always overcrowded because there are simply not enough of them. The waters in which they operate are crowded and treacherous. As a result, accidents are frequent – hundreds of lives are lost every week and the Philippines often holds the record for the greatest number of lives lost in a year, either overall or in a single accident or both. No one is sure of the death toll but in the early 1980s it was estimated that the total over the previous decade was between twenty and forty thousand.

In 1963, just off Manila Bay, the motor ferry *Juan* suffered fire and explosions in rough seas and monsoon winds. Although 401 passengers and crew were saved no one is clear just how many others were lost. Officially, sixteen bodies were recovered and a further forty-one were listed as missing, but in reality far more were lost. The same applies to the loss of the *Don Juan* in January 1980 with the loss of 'about' a thousand lives, making it the worst peacetime maritime disaster for over sixty years. The *Don Juan* had collided with a tank barge in calm seas and on a bright moonlit night. After the disaster the ship's master claimed that he had twice changed course to avoid a collision while the master of the barge claimed that it was the fault of the *Don Juan*.

Not all disasters result in a massive – or indeed any – loss of life. All the 1,164 passengers and crew on board the *Don Sulpicio* were rescued in June 1979 when fire broke out after a cigarette end had been thrown into the hold. There was panic among the passengers when the fire spread to the cabins, but the master beached the ship and she refloated on the next high tide. In May 1983 the master of the *Doña Florentina* beached his vessel on Batbatan Island so that everyone on board could be transferred safely to a sister ship.

But when the *Doña Josefina* sank off Leyte Island early in the morning of 24 April 1986 after listing and taking on water, 194 were drowned. Yet none was as bad as the sinking of the *Doña Paz* on 20 December 1987 on her way to Manila from Tacloban on the island of Leyte. This, the world's worst peacetime accident ever, killed at least 4,235 people – nearly three times the number who had died on the *Titanic*. She was not a lucky ship. This was the same ship that, under the name of *Don Sulpicio*, had already been gutted by fire. Like all the many ships sailing to and from Manila, the Visayan Islands of the Central Philippines and the southern island of Mindanão, the *Doña Paz* had to thread her way through the busy Tablas strait, a narrow eighteen-mile-wide channel between the islands. On her last voyage before Christmas, the ferry was unusually crowded, even by normal standards. Also passing through the straits was a small coastal tanker, the 600-ton *Vector* with a crew of thirteen, carrying 8,800 barrels of petroleum products. It was a run-down vessel, poorly maintained and without a lookout on the bridge. At around 10 p.m. on 20 December the *Vector* ploughed into the *Doña Paz*. The impact of an unexplained explosion amidships started a fire on both vessels, and a fireball flashed between them creating a firestorm that was fed by the highly inflammable nature of the *Vector*'s cargo. About two hours later, the *Doña Paz* sank, followed by the *Vector* two hours afterwards. Only two of the *Vector*'s crew survived and only 254 passengers from the *Doña Paz*.

According to some survivors the cabinets containing the life jackets were locked. All the thousand children on board died, and, with most of the adults, were consumed by the ferocious heat. Only 275 bodies were recovered or washed ashore.

The only vessel near enough to be of any help was the *Don Claudio*, a passenger-cargo liner. On the radar screen the officer on watch saw a floating object on fire. 'As we went along,' said the *Don Claudio*'s master, Captain Barranco, 'the bearing didn't change so I had a feeling something was wrong with that object. I summoned my chief officer, all my officers and crew and I proceeded to that area with all the lifesaving equipment ready. As we got closer I saw balls of fire something like as high as a seven-storey building. Then as we approached the scene I saw a few people around within the balls of fire so I decided to stop. I told all my officers and crew to be ready to save these people in the area. Well, I was about a mile from this flame, and I couldn't see these two ships but the flames were overwhelming. I saw the sea was on fire and it took us some time to go backwards.'

As the few survivors were brought on board, all that Captain Barranco knew was that they came from the *Doña Paz*, suffering badly from burns. Barranco radioed to his firm's head office, to the coastguard and to other vessels in the area for help. They replied, 'Later.' According to official reports it took eight hours for maritime officials to learn of the disaster and another eight hours to acquire precise information. Indeed the Manila rescue co-ordination centre did not learn of the collision until 7 a.m. on the Monday morning, nine hours later.

As is so often the case, the actual number of victims was impossible to determine. According to Yvonne Serrano Abonales, a social worker at Tacloban, there was an almost infinite number of ways of buying tickets, which greatly complicated the process of assessing the number of victims: 'Either you can buy directly in the main office of the shipping line, or from the ticket agents, the ship agents, or on the boat. Those who bought their tickets on the boat were not on the passenger list. Those who were able to get their tickets from the ticket agents and the main office were listed.' She said that the passenger list of the *Doña Paz* indicated 1,493 victims. 'However, after verification we counted 4,235 victims but after all the testimonies from relatives, there were over 5,000 victims. So far there were only 26 survivors, 24 from the *Doña Paz* and two from the MT *Vector*.'

Almost everyone in Tacloban – and, seemingly, most of the population of Leyte – knew someone on the boat. The result was chaos: 'Everybody was rushing in, rushing out. Our concern was discussing whether there were survivors or not. Every office in Tacloban had people with families on the *Doña Paz*, in the city hall, in our office, with the police. Noon-time, after the news, many of our clients were coming to our office and we had to provide them with comfort or just advice, because we were not yet sure.' As 21 December wore on, people poured in from all over the Philippines: 'Some came from Manila and then some from Samar, all over the region, from the six provinces and our 140 municipalities. I think every municipality had a victim on the *Doña Paz*. They wanted to know if there were survivors or not and where the survivors were. We could not answer them. We had to wait for the communication from Manila and our phone then was very slow, not direct dial.'

Not surprisingly, 'The atmosphere of the city was melancholy and sad during December 1987, a really big hush for the celebration of Christmas. You could see people sitting in the gutter just looking nowhere and feeling sad.' Some people didn't even know that relatives had been on board until after Christmas.

Finally the city authorities, the social services and the Red Cross combined to compile a list of everyone who claimed that a relative had been on the *Doña Paz*. Once the names had been submitted, social workers at provincial and municipal level were asked 'to assess these names, to see whether these people really took the boat and whether they were still in the area and to co-ordinate with the mayor on these identifications. Then we proceeded to the address of these victims, and checked if they were really from that place, were really missing and asked somebody if they were sure that these people went to Manila.' The checks were necessary because so many people in the slums, the *barrios*, liked to boast that they were travelling to Manila. The whole process took over a year because, as Yvonne Serrano says, 'There were people who were just taking advantage of what they could get out of the disaster.' Finally they arrived at the unsatisfactory figure of 4,235. What made matters more complicated was that at the time only heads of families were listed on the ship's passenger list: 'Other members who don't pay the fare are not included in the listing. If you have a companion below seven years old, they don't pay and cannot be listed. We always know that when the Filippinos travel, the whole family travels, including even the pigs, even the chickens.'

The official inquiry blamed the *Vector*, calling it a 'floating hazard to navigation'. Senior coastguard officials were dismissed, and sixteen other officers reassigned for having allowed the *Doña Paz* to sail when so overcrowded. Yet only nine months later the *Doña Marilyn*, which belonged to Sulpicio Line, owners of the *Doña Paz*, capsized and sank off the northwestern tip of Leyte Island during Typhoon Ruby. Battered by heavy seas, the ferry had sheltered for an hour and although the passengers had begged the captain not to venture forth he turned back and the ship was soon overwhelmed by the rough seas. Once again no one knew how many were on board – estimates varied from just over 500 to double that number. Of the total, 150 were reported dead but another 248 passengers and members of the crew were still missing a week after the disaster. President Corazón Aquino immediately suspended all the firm's other ships and announced two inquiries. The first investigated the fact that the line had sent a ferry to sea in such rough weather with passengers not on the passenger list and with an expired sea-going licence. The second inquiry was supposedly designed to ensure that in future no tickets would be issued on board such ferries, that ships would be regularly and stringently inspected, and franchises awarded only to those who did not violate these conditions. Sanctions would be applied against operators who broke the rules.

Nevertheless the accidents continued. Just before Christmas in 1988 the *Doña Conchita* caught fire in the Central Philippines, probably from fire-crackers brought illegally on board by passengers returning to the provinces from Manila for the New Year celebrations. Although some of the crew were killed, only one passenger died – from a heart attack. In 1991, all 125 passengers and 51 crew on board the *Princess Mika* were saved, but in December 1994, 145 lives were lost after another inter-island ferry, the *Cebu City*, collided with a Singaporean container carrier just outside the mouth of Manila Bay.

The death toll may diminish, but it will not disappear. However, Captain Barranco sees some improvement over the past eleven years: 'Well, now we have our traffic-separation scheme enforced by our government agencies in that area. Vigilant lookouts and competent officers are a must.' But that is easier to ask for than to achieve.

5
Beware of Greeks Offering Cruises

In one lifeboat a lady passenger pointed to a craft other than the near-est one, for which they were making. 'Do you think we could possibly organize the rowing so that we could go towards that ship?' she said, now nodding towards the more distant vessel. The tired rowers paused, looking at her in amazement. 'But why?' asked one man. 'Because it looks a much nicer one to be rescued by,' she said in all seriousness.

Geoffrey Bond, *Lakonia*, Oldbourne, London, 1966

Dangerous cruise ships are a modern phenomenon. Before 1939, cruising was confined to ships of the highest quality manned by well-qualified crews. Regrettably, as the number and size of cruise ships has increased – and con-tinues to increase – controls over their construction and manning have lagged badly behind.

The story of disasters begins with the *Lakonia*. She had been built in 1930 and named the *Johan van Oldenbarneveldt* after a Dutch statesman framed for treason. Until the 1950s, when the Dutch were chased out of what had become Indonesia, she had been used on the busy trade routes between Holland and what had been the Dutch East Indies.

She was then converted into a cruise liner, but the bulk of the money was spent on redecorating her public rooms and giving her a glossy exterior. 'She was thirty-three years old,' wrote R. A. Cahill,* 'and only two other ships of her class still in service were older . . . She was like an old beauty queen covering the ravages of age with make-up.' The result was that the more percipient passengers noted the neglect of the most elementary safety measures, especially the rotten state of the lifeboats, and the absence of a

Disasters at Sea, op. cit.

55

proper sprinkler system to cope with fire. Most became aware of faults with the electrical heating, due to the ship's refit not having been completed on time. But even if she had been properly refitted, the *Lakonia* was still a floating firetrap. As Cahill noted: 'Wood was widely used in both the construction and decoration of the cabins and public rooms, and over the years it had become liberally coated with layers of paint and varnish. Moreover a fresh coat had just been applied so the ship was literally a tinder-box.'

Late in the evening of 22 December 1963, a fire started in the barber's shop and spread rapidly. At 11.30 p.m., little more than half an hour after it had broken out, the captain had stopped the vessel, or so he said, although some passengers claim that the ship was still under way. The launch of the lifeboats varied from farce to disaster. 'Some boats tipped up,' wrote Geoffrey Bond, 'some fell askew, some successfully and smoothly reached the water. Four lifeboats remained stuck in their davits, the heat of the fire being too intense to allow their release.' Indeed, some could not be launched because chains jammed or had rusted. 'There was no planned smoothness about any part of the operation', continued Bond. One boat with a capacity for eighty passengers contained only one officer and seven members of the crew, who somehow proved incapable of rescuing anyone else. The ship, which was nominally Greek, carried a largely inexperienced crew of a dozen nationalities, including Cypriots, Dutch, Germans, British, Canadians, French, Belgians and Chinese. Some escaped early and by no means empty-handed. The chief steward warned passengers of looting and, as Geoffrey Bond says, 'It is hard to explain away the quantity of jewellery in the pockets of one drowned steward.' Most of the lifeboats started to ship water because the bungs were missing, and two hundred passengers remained on the ship rather than risk using them.

The master, Captain Mathios Zarbis, was ill-equipped to cope with an emergency. 'No doubt,' noted Cahill drily, 'he was picked for the job as much for his convivial nature as for his professional qualifications.' To be fair, he was the last to leave his stricken ship on the following afternoon.

The captain's request for help had soon been answered – although he experienced difficulty in warning the passengers since the public-address system wouldn't work. But perhaps the worst problem encountered in saving them from the sinking ship was that there had been only the most notional emergency drills. Also – and this is so with most cruise ships – the passengers tended to be elderly and by no means sprightly or bold enough to skip up rope-ladders or jump from boat to boat.

To make matters worse, neither of the first two ships on the scene, the British freighter *Montcalm* and the Argentinian freighter *Salta*, dared come too close for fear of hitting lifeboats or rafts. Nevertheless, as dawn came up they started to pick up survivors. The Argentinian seamen proved particularly expert in lassoing those in the sea. Another rescuer, the Pakistani freighter *Mehdi*, performed heroically too. Other ships proved less helpful; indeed, the captain of the American freighter *Rio Grande* was seemingly unwilling to launch a lifeboat, although his crew were a tower of strength. The biggest and best-equipped vessel in the area, the American liner *Independence*, did not come near the scene and soon resumed course towards Casablanca.

The most remarkable fact of the *Lakonia* catastrophe was the number of survivors: despite the heat from the fire and the chaos in which the ship was abandoned 'only' 98 of the 646 passengers died and 30 of the 376 crew.

Over the past twenty years, as the cruise business has boomed, offering every type of holiday from a day out devoted to gambling to months voyaging round the world, the opportunity for accidents has multiplied accordingly, particularly as so many of the boats – especially those owned by the lesser Greek shipping companies – are old and inadequately equipped. (Some of the most decrepit carry the name 'Scandinavian' in an attempt to assure potential customers of their reliability.) Unfortunately, the international regulators have proved unable to foresee – or to do anything about – the ever-increasing dangers.

The analysis by Norman Hooke* of cruise ships lost in the thirty-three years since the sinking of the *Lakonia* shows: first, the losses occurred overwhelmingly among older ships, the average age of which was twenty-seven. (The worst disaster involved a ship that was sixty-one years old. In 1986 the Russian cruise ship *Admiral Nakhimov* collided with a bulk carrier on a short cruise on the Black Sea from Odessa to Batum, killing 423 of the nearly 900 people aboard.) But two-thirds of the losses were the result of fires, some started by arsonists, and five occurred while the ship involved was in harbour or, more usually, undergoing repairs in dry dock.

Nationality also played a key role in a ship's fate. Of the twenty-seven cases cited by Hooke, three each were registered in Russia and the

---

Maritime Casualties, 1963–1996, Norman Hooke, LLP, London, 1997.

Bahamas, two were Italian and five each Liberian and Greek.

The worst record is probably that of the Epirotiki Line, which lost three vessels in three years. All had been renamed more than once; all had more or less eventful lives. On 21 October 1988 its motor ship *Jupiter* (ex-*Moledet*, ex-*Alexandros*) sank after being hit by an Italian motor-vehicle carrier, the *Adige*. It had just sailed from Piraeus on a cruise through the eastern Mediterranean, carrying mainly British schoolchildren and their teachers. Partly because the ship took over an hour to sink, partly because the weather was good and the sea calm, only four people died out of a total of nearly 600 on board.

The *Adige* and its captain, Flavio Caminale, were clearly to blame for the disaster: the master had pulled his ship away from the *Jupiter* immediately after the two vessels had collided, opening up a hole in the side of his ship. After a lengthy delay, and much disagreement, the Greek official report blamed both captains (as well as the Piraeus signal station, which had not been able to identify the *Adige*). Four years after the collision, Captain Caminale was finally convicted for his part in the loss of the *Jupiter*. He was sentenced to six years' imprisonment on a variety of charges, but the judge carefully left a loophole: he kept each individual sentence to less than two years, enabling the accused to stay out of prison by paying a small fine (in this case a mere $7,000), a common practice in Greece when courts decide that the circumstances of a case warrant leniency.

Three years later the Epirotiki Line lost the *Pegasus*. Like so many other such vessels, she had shuttled between owners, sometimes after accidents. Originally called the *Ionian Express*, she was a 13,000-ton ro-ro ferry built in a French yard in 1975. Nine years later, under the name of *Sundancer*, she had partially sunk after striking rocks off Vancouver Island while on a cruise from Vancouver to Alaska. There was no loss of life, but she was adjudged a 'constructive total loss', then sold. In 1991, while being used as an exhibition ship under the name *Pegasus*, she suffered a fire and was adjudged a loss for a second time. She was then sold by Epirotiki and was being converted for use as a luxury ferry, either in the Baltic or in the Irish Sea, when she was finally gutted by fire, sold to Turkish ship-breakers and demolished.

On 4 August 1991 another Epirotiki vessel, the forty-year-old cruise ship *Oceanos* (ex-*Jean Laborde*, ex-*Mykinai*, ex-*Eastern Princess*) set off in a force-13 gale from Durban, South Africa, with sailors bailing out water from the verandahs on the main deck. However, their efforts were in vain and the ship soon began to sink. They sent a Mayday signal at 2300 on 3 August, advising that the vessel was leaking and that one watertight compartment was flooded. At 0200 they reported that the engine room was flooded and although two lifeboats were afloat bad weather was preventing any others being launched. Most of the 374 passengers who took to the boats were rescued by nearby ships. At daylight, thirteen helicopters from the South African Defence Force began lifting 180 people from the ship in gale conditions.

The rescue was chaotic. The captain took off in the first helicopter, so members of the band took charge of co-ordinating the rescue, helping winchmen as the ship continued to roll and sink. In one bizarre incident the man in charge of the ship's casino went back to rescue the cash, then slipped off the winch and drifted for nine hours before being picked up. Yet, in the end, all 580 aboard were rescued. The Greek inquiry found the master and four of the ship's officers responsible for not closing watertight doors in time and for not preventing water from a damaged pipeline flooding the rest of the vessel, leading to progressive loss of stability.

But perhaps the story that provides every sort of experience known to a cruise liner and its unfortunate passengers is that of the *Achille Lauro*. It dates back to 1939 when the ship was laid down in the Dutch port of Flushing. Work on her stopped during the war and was resumed in 1945 after The Netherlands had been liberated. The vessel's first name was *Willem Ruys*, after a former director of the Royal Rotterdam Lloyd Line who had been executed by the Germans, a suitably morbid start for what proved a long and miserable history. She began by running between The Netherlands and the Dutch East Indies, but after independence she was employed as an ordinary passenger liner of the sort that speedily became obsolete with the rapid growth of jet travel in the early 1960s.

In 1964 she was withdrawn from service and a year later was sold to the Italian Lauro line, which renamed her *Achille Lauro*. While she was undergoing major reconstruction in Palermo, the liner was devastated by fire, which destroyed much of the accommodation. After a short spell plying between Southampton and Australia, she was commissioned as a cruise liner. In 1972 she suffered another severe fire, due to arson, while undergoing modernization, this time in Genoa. This caused her to list 10 degrees and resulted in damage similar to that which she had sustained eight years earlier.

No sooner had she returned to service than the crew walked out in protest at the allegedly poor conditions on board. They were led by the chief engineer, who claimed that the machinery in the engine room was faulty. The passengers – impoverished emigrants on their way to Australia and New Zealand – were stranded for five days in Tenerife, living off a meagre food allowance before a scratch crew was assembled to replace those who had left in disgust.

In 1975, the *Achille Lauro* collided with a livestock carrier off the coast of Turkey, killing all the cattle aboard and a member of the crew. In 1982 there was another fire and, although the crew extinguished it, two elderly passengers died of heart attacks. The next year the ship was placed under arrest when her owners ran into financial difficulties. Two years later, she sailed again after she had changed hands.

Despite her long and troubled career, the *Achille Lauro* first came to the world's attention when she was hijacked off Port Said on 7 October 1985 by four Palestinian commandos who had posed as passengers. They threatened to blow up the vessel unless the Israeli government freed fifty Palestinian prisoners being held in Israel. Two days later following a peace parlay on board, the gunmen left the ship – and left behind the body of a disabled sixty-nine-year-old American passenger, Leon Klinghoffer, killed when they had taken the vessel over in a hail of gunfire.

As a result the Americans forced the Boeing 737 airliner carrying the hijackers to land at an airbase in Sicily where they were formally charged with terrorist offences. During their trial it emerged that they had planned to attack the ship while she was in port and had been forced into premature action when a steward discovered weapons in their cabin.

In 1986 the *Achille Lauro* ran aground on a sandbank at the entrance to the port of Alexandria. In 1994 her troubled life came to an end, by which time she was one of the ten oldest ocean-going cruise liners still in commercial use. Fire broke out in the engine-room just after midnight on 30 November while she was off the coast of Somalia on a three-week cruise from Genoa through the Suez Canal to Durban. She was carrying 577 passengers and a crew of 402 – including some members of the band from the *Oceanos*. Most of the passengers were either in their cabins or enjoying a black-tie ball.

The fire raged out of control in the stern, then spread through the vessel, partially gutting her. The passengers were assembled on the deck for seven hours while the crew fought the blaze, but so much water was poured on to the flames that the ship began to list heavily. The passengers and most of the crew took to the lifeboats while about a hundred crew members remained on board in a vain attempt to put out the flames. In the end they, too, had to abandon ship when the fire went out of control. Large numbers of vessels raced to the scene and in a remarkable rescue effort only four of the 979 people aboard died. All were elderly. One was killed by a blow to the head as he attempted to board a lifeboat, two died from unspecified illnesses and one was listed as missing. Rescue was not, however, the end of their ordeal. Most of those on board were picked up by a bulk carrier, the *Hawaiian King*, which for the next twenty-four hours coped with nearly a thousand survivors on a ship with accommodation and facilities for fifty.

The major source of disasters to cruise ships, both historic and future, lies in the ever-growing number of cruises undertaken from the United States, above all from southern Florida. There, the cruise industry has been on a steady climb since a television series set on a cruise ship, *Love Boat*, enjoyed a brief period of success in the late 1970s. The cruises vary from gamblers' or gourmets' one-day 'cruises to nowhere', to voyages taking in much of the Caribbean.

The underlying problem is simple. It costs a fortune to build and man a ship capable of fulfilling the strict rules laid down for vessels flying the American flag. As a result there are only three such cruise ships, all operating out of Hawaii. All those sailing from Miami, Fort Lauderdale and the other Florida ports are registered under flags of convenience, and often owned by shadowy companies that disappear behind legal smoke screens at the first sign of trouble. Moreover, companies operating the day cruises have in the past succeeded in using a loophole in international law designed to prevent over-regulation of smaller ships.

These floating slums – not too strong a word for vessels some of whose lack of elementary hygiene leads to regular bouts of gastroenteritis among the passengers – operate with a hotchpotch of crews, who often do not share a common language. In 1966 two passengers died when fire destroyed the *Viking Princess* off Cuba. In 1979 the *Bohème* burned while docked at Miami and in 1980 the passengers and crew of the *Prinsendam* had a lucky escape when their ship caught fire and sank off the coast of Alaska. All 524 people on board were rescued – although many of the generally elderly passengers had to wait in the lifeboats for over thirteen hours before being picked up. Less than a day later a fierce storm hit the area.

The problems on 'phoney' cruise ships – those without any destination or purpose other than to allow their passengers to gamble, eat and drink – are exacerbated by their organization. As Captain Paul Esbensen of the NTSB explains: 'Most of the gambling and the rooms and everything else are concessions. So those people who come aboard to serve in the dining room and everywhere else are not truly seamen. The number of real seamen on these ships, the operating crew, are very limited. The biggest portion of the so-called crew on the ship is for the gambling and hotel staff, and people who handle the restaurants.'

His criticisms could apply to many disasters. For example fire broke out in the auxiliary generator room of the Bahamian-registered *Scandinavian Sun* just before midnight on 20 August 1984 shortly after it had docked in Miami. It had just completed its daily fourteen-hour cruise to Freeport in the Bahamas with 530 passengers and 201 crew. The fire was caused by the crew's failure to tighten a threaded pipe fitting on the lubricating-oil line of a diesel generator, allowing it to spray oil which then caught fire. The crew also failed to shut the watertight door and the self-closing fire doors between the engine room and the passenger accommodation. There was no fire-alarm watch and no safety drills for passengers. Four people died.

As we have seen from the story of the *Achille Lauro*, the operators of these potential deathtraps very often try to ensure that a single disaster does not necessarily mean total loss. That same year, 1984, the *Scandinavian Sea* was on her way back to Port Canaveral after her regular daily 'cruise to nowhere' when an inflammable liquid was poured (or spilt – it is still not clear whether the fire was the result of an accident or arson) on to the floor of one of the crew's staterooms at about 7.30 p.m. The fire was discovered by two of the crew who didn't realize that a fire hydrant and a powerful hose-pipe were nearby. When efforts were made to douse the fire the master removed the only qualified officer from the scene of the fire to help him moor the boat.

The crew's attempts to put out the blaze were also hampered by the fact that they did not know each other, that no single person was in charge and that they had no protective clothing. Only minor injuries were suffered but the fire raged out of control, gutting nearly a third of the ship. The accommodation was badly damaged while several decks buckled in the intensity of the heat. When he arrived the next morning, Paul Esbensen found that 'The ship was still burning and the fire departments, or various trucks on the pier, were baling water into it'.

In theory, the fire should not have spread. As Esbensen explains: 'Ships are designed to survive fires. Within the ship, of course, you have the fire-extinguishing system, and passenger ships have separate zones so you can isolate fires. This particular ship had a number of zones; there were both horizontal and vertical zones separated by decks. The ventilation system is designed to be automatically shut down when fire is found in a zone. Had the ship had to respond to this fire offshore *without* coming to the pier, I imagine that they would have had the fire out because the ship's crew was trained in fire-fighting. Now, I believe that one of the reasons they decided to bring the ship in was because of her proximity to the port – it was only nine miles away. So they brought the ship in to get rid of the people. The primary responsibility of any ship's officers or the master of the ship is for the passengers. In this case he's close enough to get the ship into the pier and get the passengers off, which was the biggest hurdle he had to cross. And he did that successfully, and everybody agreed that it was the proper move. The only thing is, that's where it broke down. From then on when the shoreside fire-fighters came aboard, the ship's personnel did not assist in fighting the fire or direct them into the ship's systems.

'The ship has systems with fire hoses and fire pumps and they could have had fire hoses running right away.' But as he discovered when he tried to find out who was directing operations, 'I saw the ship's officers, the master and the rest of the crew, sitting on the pier. And I was quite surprised to see them down there. I said, "Is anybody directing the fire-fighters aboard the ship so they know where they're going?" Their response was that it was the coastguard's responsibility. The coastguard said, "No, we don't put fires out, we'll assist and we'll oversee things but we certainly don't have the manpower or the equipment to come down."'

As a result, 'The responsibility at that time was assumed supposedly by the local fire departments. And they didn't have the expertise to fight marine fires. We noticed a lot of damage to the ship that was caused by the addressing of the fire by the fire departments. They were just volunteer fire departments from the various communities round there.' If there had been someone in the port who had known about fighting fire on board ship then the blaze could have been contained. Thanks to the NTSB's report on the fire, this gap has now been filled. The report included the usual catalogue of inadequacies: no protective clothing was worn, there was no sprinkler system, many of the furnishings were not fire retardant, and those that were generated too much smoke. The crew could not have evacuated the passengers if the fire had occurred at sea. The captain was negligent.

The ship was eventually declared a 'constructive loss' and sold for a mere $600,000 to what are described as 'Greek interests'. Subsequently, she was sold at a considerable profit to American buyers who renamed her the *Venus Venturer* and repaired her. She was then detained because of legal problems before she started a new life as a gambling ship, named *Discovery 1*, two years after the fire.

But problems are not confined to ships run by dubious operators. As cruise ships grow ever larger and move into new and often uncharted waters, they create fresh problems, especially if they take a cavalier approach to their new circumstances. This is not a new phenomenon. In 1971 the 20,000-ton French liner *Antilles* ran aground on an uncharted reef off Princess Margaret's holiday island, Mustique, opening a hole along two of her holds. The master decided to jettison fuel while waiting for rescue vessels and to try to lift the liner off the reef. Unfortunately the fuel caught fire and he had to give the order to abandon ship.

One of the vessels that raced to help the *Antilles* was the *QE2*, the pride of Cunard's fleet, which itself ran aground in Vineyard Sound off the coast of Massachusetts on 7 August 1993. The weather was fine and both the master and the pilot felt confident enough to increase her speed to 24 knots, but just before 10 p.m. she grounded. Over 400 feet of the ship's 963-foot hull had been damaged and seven of her double-bottomed tanks holed. The damage cost Cunard $50 million in repairs and lost income as well as causing untold embarrassment.

The accident was down to the usual mixture of human and technical error, but as the NTSB investigator Leon Katcharian pointed out, it need not have happened had the captain and the pilot communicated properly. 'The pilot had been aboard all this time,' says Katcharian, 'but he had not met with the navigator or the master to determine what track the vessel would take leaving Vineyard Sound. At a critical point you could turn left to go south of the shoaling area where it grounded, or you could pass round to the north of it. The captain and the crew of the *QE2* had in mind which way they were going to leave the area, and the pilot had in his mind the way he would leave the area, but they never discussed the situation. As they travelled down Vineyard Sound, the pilot decided he was going to pass round north of the shoaling area to get to where he would be dropped off. After they cleared the anchorage and small-boat traffic, they travelled at 25 knots to leave Vineyard Sound . . . At a certain point the pilot then decided to turn to the west and go above the point where the vessel eventually grounded. The person navigating advised his senior officer, and the officer advised the captain of the track that the vessel would be taking and the possible shoaling area, seven miles ahead of them. The master passed the word down to the pilot that he wanted to pass south of this area, and the pilot changed course.

'One of the problems was that they didn't know exactly where they were when they changed course, and the course took them right over the shoaling area which was set on the charts at 39 feet. When you look at a chart there's a date on it, and you assume a 1990 chart or 1991 chart is right up to date, but we discovered at the hearing that many of the soundings along the East Coast of the United States were approximately fifty years old, except for the more heavily travelled areas. The methods of taking the soundings and depths used on the chart were a lot different than they are today. They covered smaller areas and were generalized. Nowadays when you survey the bottom you have much more accuracy and placement of more dangers. The distance between the tracks that the vessel used was 400 yards and the narrowness of the [radar] beams or the sounding devices really limited the information gathered. But one reason for this accident could have been that the pilot was not consulted for six or seven hours as to what track the vessel would take before leaving the anchorage.'

An underwater survey identified a number of rocks on the seabed with paint and metal embedded in them. Tests matched the samples to the *QE2*'s hull: there could be no doubt that she had hit the bottom. The ship had a draught of 32 feet, yet at its shallowest the water through which the pilot was navigating was 39 feet. The levels were measured, the charts checked and echo soundings confirmed their validity.

The cause of this anomaly was a phenomenon known as 'squat'. This had been identified at the turn of the century and refers to the different directions taken by the water displaced by the passage of a ship. At the bow the water is pushed forward but further back it starts to flow aft until just behind the stern when it begins to close inward and upward, moving slightly forward at the same time. As this happens the water level – and with it the ship – is lowered. The phenomenon is particularly noticeable in restricted waterways, and increases with the speed of a vessel.

Although it had been calculated that squat could be as much as 16 feet where supertankers were concerned, the consensus prevailing when the *QE2* grounded was that squat could not explain what had happened. However, Ash Chatterjee, an investigator with the NTSB, spotted that the calculations in the textbooks applied exclusively to ships moving at the relatively slow speeds that most mariners would adopt when navigating tricky, shallow channels. Under these circumstances squat was reckoned to be between one and two feet. Chatterjee realized that the *QE2* had not been sailing slowly.

Having worked out that the damage to the *QE2*'s hull was too great to be explained by the usual mathematical formulae he went back to first principles. He calculated that the shallowness of the water would also have greatly increased the effect of the squat experienced by the ship. The combination of speed and shallowness meant that the squat amounted to an unheard-of eight feet – a new worry for passengers and crew on large cruise liners.

6
Fire and Water: a Fatal Mixture?

When the President of the National Transport Safety Association asked one crew member what they should do in the event of fire he told us he could get us ice, soap or towels.

Anon

Two recent stories of fires aboard ships – the *All Alaskan*, a fish-processing vessel, and the *Scandinavian Star*, a ro-ro ferry – provide a startling contrast, showing that even the most severe fire need not prove fatal if the crew is competent and well trained. The tragic story of the *Star* provides object lessons in everything from the material used in a ship to the need for proper inspections, a competent crew who speak the same language and, above all, for the ability to trace and hold responsible the shadowy men and companies who control too many of the world's ships.

At first sight the *All Alaskan* does not look like an exemplar of safety. It takes crab from the fishing-boats off Alaska and, as one of the crew, Brent Reid, explains: 'The processors would butcher the crabs and separate the legs from the bodies. Then they would be cooked, packed, boxed, frozen. Most of the crab was sent to Japan.' It is not well policed – virtually none of the 250 fish-processing vessels operating in American waters are inspected.

On the 24 July 1994 it was a long time, up to eight and a half hours, from when the fire started to when the hold began to exude a strange smell and the alarm was given. Leon Katcharian of the NTSB explains why. 'On these fish-processing vessels the majority of the people could be fish processors who have little or no marine experience. Their safety is dependent upon the deck-hands and the ship's officers. And in such a situation we believe that these fire teams should be trained in marine fire-fighting and not just learn it from on-the-job training, because there are a lot of people who they're responsible for, similar to a passenger ship where there are a lot of passengers who generally don't have any experience in fires.'

Nevertheless the proper precautions seem to have been taken. According to Brent Reid: 'We had people walking through the ship at all times, twenty-four hours a day, whenever we were at sea. They were called firewatchers and apparently whoever was on the fire-watch at that time had walked through the cargo holds and noticed that there was a peculiar smell in one of them.' Unfortunately, although one of the processors then reported the strange smell to their immediate supervisors, 'The people on the bridge or in the wheelhouse were never notified,' says Katcharian. 'The master or the chief mate who had been on watch were never notified. And the way it was explained is that there are many odours on a ship and the engineer is always looking for them, but the master said that if he had been advised he would have stopped the vessel and made a much more thorough inspection.' Nevertheless, 'As soon as the captain was advised that there was a fire, he sounded the general alarm to get people to their fire stations and to their abandon-ship stations. He realized that the fire was out of control. Within less than an hour he notified the coastguard that they would be abandoning ship. His decision turned out to be correct. The ship burned for another three or four days. And the crew was fortunate. It was very calm ocean conditions, and there were other vessels close by to help people get off the ship. They didn't have to go into life-rafts, although a few did temporarily, but they were directly placed on vessels and on barges, so they got away from the danger pretty quickly.'

It helped, says Brent Reid, that 'the captain had positioned the boat so that the wind was blowing off the bow. No smoke would come aft where everybody was. During the whole evacuation all the smoke went directly out of the bow or off the starboard side of the ship. Everybody was in survival suits. People started coming down the ladders, all the life-rafts had been launched, they were tied to the rail and they were surrounding the stern of the boat. We put the Jacob's ladders [emergency rope ladders] down, people started down them then the tug got there.

'Everybody was very calm. Nobody thought they were in danger – in fact, everybody was more worried about if their buddy had a pack of cigarettes or something. There was just a handful of people that thought maybe there was a person missing, who hadn't returned from below.' In fact, not everyone was calm. Beverley Morgan, who had been working in the galley, describes how she 'went over the side on a Jacob's ladder and went down into my designated lifeboat. My room-mate, who I shared a cabin with on the boat, came after me and she had a little bit of a problem getting down the ladder. She fell into the water and panicked when we were trying to pull her into the raft. The captain was giving directions quite loudly to make sure we got her in there. So that was one of the worst incidents for me during the whole evacuation. The ship was listing quite a bit, looked like it was going to just tip over in the water. It was pretty scary when I realized how close we were to it. Looking up from the water level, you realize how big it is. It was listing so bad I felt that if it were to sink we wouldn't have a chance, we'd be pulled under with it. So we just cut the line and oared out as fast as we could to get away from it.'

Reid explains the relative lack of tension: 'It was daylight, the seas were very calm, everything was extremely organized. Everybody was single file, nobody was worried about not getting into a raft. Everybody could see that there was a tug fairly close to help, the coastguard was hovering above us in a helicopter in case anybody happened to fall into the water. Nobody really felt that their lives were in danger at all.' They were well prepared too, because the captain had insisted on proper fire drills. They would put on fire suits, 'he would give us a list of fire extinguishers, fire stations, make us find them and report back to him where they were. He's just very hard about fires and how the worst thing that could ever happen to you while you're on a boat is to have a fire break out.'

Beverley Morgan agrees: 'The fire drills helped a lot in preparing us for this incident. Everybody was well informed as to where their stations were, their primary evacuation routes. We drilled quite often and in fact we had one the day before.'

In the event only one person was lost. As Katcharian explains, 'The two watch-keepers heard the fire and then they ran down to the locker, put on oxygen-breathing apparatus and protective clothing, took one fire extinguisher and ran to the scene. Now, normally before they would do such a thing, they would be instructed as to what procedures to follow. They would have back-up teams with fire hoses and proceed from there. On this day, they went down to the scene and they opened the door to the lower hold. They felt heat coming out, and then all of a sudden flames started coming out the door. And they were not able to re-close it. The more experienced person was able to escape but the less experienced man got confused in the maze of fish-processing equipment, lost his friend, and was found dead in the area near where the fire emanated from the door.'

The damage was enormous, partly because of the explosion of bottles of ammonia and acetylene, but it did not take the NTSB's investigators long to work out the sequence of events. The scene of the outbreak, says Leon Katcharian, 'was a freezer hold where the temperature was approximately –26°F. Looking round, we narrowed it down to a drainpipe from a refrigeration system evaporator. And then we looked around to see what sources of ignition were present and we looked at electrical connections. There was a heating pad underneath the drainpipe from the evaporator that led to another larger drainpipe.' It had wires wrapped around it and we compared that to drainpipes that did not have any damage. We noticed that, unlike the undamaged sample, all the insulation had been burned away from this drainpipe. There was a hot spot on the steel bulkhead next to where this drainpipe was, and the wires on that particular drainpipe had been broken. When they were examined in our lab we noted that they had been beaded, which gives an indication that they had shorted and could possibly have caused a spark.

'The next thing we looked at was the combustible materials in the area. This cargo hold had spray-on rigid polyurethane foam on all the bulkheads and overhead as an insulation material. Once this type of insulation starts burning it's very difficult to put out, and in this case we surmised that the heat tape* had sparked, had burned through the insulation that had been around it and from there had penetrated that insulation and had eventually worked its way to an unprotected foam on the bulkhead, which was close to where the drainpipe was. Once a spark or anything gets to the polyurethane it'll heat, it'll melt and then vaporize and start burning. It burns very hot and very rapidly, producing a lot of black smoke and carbon monoxide' – also giving off a strong and disagreeable smell.

Brent Reid adds: 'When you're stacking product you try to utilize as much space as possible. I don't believe at this particular time that we were totally full, but apparently there was some product stacked up against some of the pipes, and my understanding is that one of the bags had ruptured the heat tape which, I guess, caused it to spark and set some of the bags on fire.'

*A special, electrically heated type of tape used in extremely cold conditions to prevent water from freezing in pipes like the fuel pipes in a refrigerated ship.

To Beverley Morgan all was not sweetness and light. Many of her colleagues were 'totally devastated. A lot of the people who work on the vessel, that is their home, they live there, their belongings were there. We all left the vessel with nothing, no identification, no money, no change of clothing, nothing. It would be the same as if you came home and your house had burned down and you lost everything.'

But at least only one of the crew of the *All Alaskan* had lost his life. By contrast, 158 unfortunates died on board the *Scandinavian Star*, which caught fire on 7 April 1990 while on a voyage across the Skagerrak from Oslo to Frederikshavn in northern Denmark. She had already suffered one fire while sailing in the Gulf of Mexico in 1988, six weeks after an inspection by coastguard officials had shown that all the twenty-one smoke alarms in the engine room were out of order. The fire could have been brought under control immediately if any member of the crew had had the knowledge – or the nerve – to shut down the fuel supply. Indeed, a Honduran motorman had wanted to do so but felt that he lacked authority to take such drastic action. When he tried to tell the Filippino engineer in the control room the two spoke different languages and had to communicate through hand signals. Eventually, though, the fire was brought under control – but none of the recommendations made by the NTSB after the inquiry was implemented.

In 1990 the *Star* was transferred to Danish registry and immediately started sailing between Norway and Denmark. The fatal voyage was clearly a mess from the start, as many of the passengers realized. Jan Harsem was twenty-nine, his wife Christine twenty-four and they had been married for two and a half years. They had an eighteen-month-old son, Halvor, and Christine was pregnant again. They had rented a small cabin on the west coast of Denmark for Easter. As they drove to the ferry, 'We were singing in the car, we were looking forward to the Easter holiday. We came to the harbour in Oslo and we saw there was a mess in the booking department. The ship was delayed.'

When Torbjorn Kalberg and his family went on board they found the ship 'looking more like a construction site than a ship, and we were quite puzzled because it took so long to get on board. The girls working with the cabins said "there is a Danish Mafia taking over everything here and we don't have any cabins to give to you because the keys don't match."' They were waiting for their cabin keys in the restaurant, when they had an alarming experience: 'One of our party was trying to do something with the lamps on top of our table. One of the crew came and said not to do it because yesterday there had been quite an explosion. We were a bit frightened.'

In the early hours of 7 April the *Star* caught fire in calm seas while carrying 383 passengers and a crew of 98. It did not help, as Paul Esbensen of the NTSB pointed out, that there had been no fire drills, although the crew knew their duties in an emergency. When the fire broke out the Kalbergs managed to get on to the deck. 'We just waited for twenty minutes and we heard on the loudspeaker that everything was under control. Then we saw the *Stena Saga* [another ferry] and we were told that we would soon be safe. We climbed the ladder up to the top deck and people were running around half naked, looking for their friends and relatives. The lifeboats were already beginning to fill up and no one knew how to launch them. I think one boat was hanging the wrong way and people were frightened that they would fall into the water.' The combination of rescue helicopters and ferries, plus the lifeboats, reduced the death toll – at least among those who made it on to the deck. But many didn't.

When the Harsems woke, Christine told Jan to carry the baby. Jan describes what happened. 'I took Halvor in my arms and went out of the cabin and came into the corridor. I couldn't see anything, there was so much smoke, I couldn't even see the wall at the other side.' At the same moment 'there was some strange noise going through the whole corridor and then the light went out and it was totally dark. I was trapped in this corridor but I started walking and I came out in the fresh air again. It was night and I could see the stars. Then I tried to go back where I had come from to look for Christine but there was so much smoke. It was dark and it was very strong, like a powerful waterfall coming out from all the openings in the ship.'

Jan and Halvor were soon rescued by the *Stena Saga*, and Jan 'hoped that perhaps Christine was on board another ship. But when I came back to Oslo I understood that the worst may have happened but I didn't want to think these thoughts. I was with Halvor and I cried a lot. One week later, the confirmation came that she was found on board and she was dead.'

The truth behind this tragedy was so simple as to be almost unbearable. When Christine walked down the corridor she must have turned left into the path of the smoke and been asphyxiated. When Jan, with Halvor in his arms, followed a few moments later, he turned right at the same junction, virtually straight into the safety of the open air on the deck. Esbensen explains how if someone had opened the door at the end of the passageway down which Christine walked, she could have got out on to the open deck, but on the door it said Crew Only.

Unfortunately, says Esbensen, 'The passageways were not well marked so that everybody could recognize them. The smoke in one of the main passageways had come down so low that the safety signs were obliterated. In this long passageway we found seventy people.' Later, Kjerll Schmidt Pedersen, one of the inquiry investigators, 'discovered that some of the crew were actually sleeping a few decks below the car deck. The fire was going from the car deck upwards. At seven or eight o'clock in the morning they were awake and asked what all the fuss was about. They were quite safe underneath the fire.'

The confusion surrounding the disaster was compounded because eighty of the crew were new to the vessel and were Portuguese or Filippino, which created considerable language and communication problems. Professor Stenn Erichsen, another of the investigators, noted how 'a very good manning agency had been approached by the company who was operating the ship and had refused to participate in the manning because the time to find an appropriate crew and acquaint them with the ship was too short.' But, as Kalberg says, the crew shouldn't be blamed for the chaos: 'I think they were trying to calm people down even if they themselves were a bit scared. I think later on they were criticized for doing bad work but on this ship where everything was disorganized and the support from the land-based organization was lacking, I think it would be unfair to blame the inexperienced crew for not behaving professionally.'

The master, Hugo Larsen – who, incidentally, left before all the passengers had been taken off – suspected arson: three different fires had started at three different spots all involving piles of clothing. Two were quickly extinguished but the third took hold and spread rapidly. The ship was towed into the Swedish port of Lysekil where the fire was finally put out. The three decks above the car deck were damaged and the car deck itself was completely burned out. A heap of bodies was found on the restaurant deck towards the bow, and numbers of others in cabins.

And the arsonist? Pedersen does not think that the culprit was aware of what he was starting: 'No one could imagine that these walls could be ignited and burn and have a self-sustained fire as was the case. I think that he wanted to make a nuisance only. After all, the guy in question was also going to bed in his cabin and he would be one of the victims of the fire.'

A commission of inquiry was soon set up. Professor Erichsen tells the story: it was due to a 'sad set of circumstances. The fire started in a part of the ship where there were no passengers, no crew, and the fire alarm was given for a part of the ship where the fire did not start. The officers on watch on the bridge did not know where the fire was so they started to close the fire doors automatically from the bridge. This closure was not quite appropriate. There was no automatic monitoring of fire or smoke on that ship, and there was no sprinkler system. If either had been there the officers on the bridge would have known where the fire started.'

Because the fire started in an unmanned part of the ship, says Pedersen, 'the doors were left open into the staircase into the passenger deck, it was open all through to the other side. By accident it was also open into the car deck because the fire door was blocked open.' The ventilation system on the ship worked by letting air into the cabins and expelling the excess into the corridors. When the captain closed the fire doors the flow was boosted tenfold into the open corridors, as well as in the corridor where the fire started. 'By closing the doors,' says Pedersen, 'the captain, without knowing it, helped the fire to grow very rapidly.

'When the ventilation system was turned off, the smoke penetrated into the cabins and killed people there too.'

Erichsen points out another unhappy design feature, the one that killed Christine Harsem. The corridors of the ship ensured that 'some passengers were trapped in a dead end. It was a poor design, perhaps because of the installation of a swimming-pool or something.'

As with aircraft, the materials used in the furniture and fittings of a ship can help to convert a drama into a catastrophe. Pedersen says, 'The walls were not fireproof in every sense. They were fireproof in the sense that a fire would not work itself through the walls, but they were covered with some plastic material which caught fire and that was what happened where they had set these [bags of clothes] on fire.'

Paul Esbensen explains: 'Although the materials used in the cabins and all the bulkheads in the cabins, the panels, were fireproof, the overlay was vinyl [which] burns quite rapidly and generated much of the smoke.'

The plastic laminate used to line the corridors played a crucial role. 'Large amounts of hydrogen cyanide were released by burning this plastic laminate,' says Pedersen, 'more than we could ever expect from such material and we guessed that most of that came from the melamine surface of the lining.' The investigators' experiments proved that the concentration was such that 'If you stayed just one minute in that type of concentration you would be dead. That's the fatal limit.' There was also a great deal of carbon monoxide. 'In this fire the hydrogen cyanide present in the smoke gave a knock-down effect, which with the carbon monoxide got the people out of action or control very quickly. The cabin-lining material had been tested, but only for the density of smoke it produced. It is only since the fire that they have to be tested for the density of the seven toxic gases produced in a fire.'

Once Jan Harsem had begun to get over the shock, he joined the support group of survivors campaigning for improved safety standards: the official report on the disaster had concluded that the ship should never have sailed, and made thirty or forty recommendations – including the installation of sprinkler systems, which will not be compulsory until 2005. The delay angers Harsem: 'The Norwegian community and city of Lillehammer needed five years from when they heard the decision that they would host the Winter Olympics until the Olympics took place. The ship-owners need fifteen years to put water-sprinkling systems on board their ships. That's crazy.'

The disaster raised some fundamental questions, about control, inspection and, above all, ownership. As Harsem says: 'Ships should be controlled by the countries between which they are sailing, not by the country in which they are registered, which may well have no control at all.' (Erichsen found it extraordinary that 'There was a new ship in the service but there was no routine for the Oslo port authority to report to the maritime authority.') 'The *Scandinavian Star* was put into service without any inspection at all,' says Harsem. 'In my opinion, the ship was transferred from the Caribbean to the Scandinavian sea because the ship-owners knew that in Scandinavia there are only a few inspections of these ships, and if there is an inspection they just rely on the certificates from the classification society and from the flag state. In this case the flag state made no inspection at all. The classification society was also responsible for the flag-state inspections and in international shipping classification societies are paid by the ship-owners. I must say I don't trust the inspection authorities.'

But the most fundamental flaw in the international shipping scene brought into the open by the efforts of Harsem and his colleagues concerned the question of ownership of ships. As Harsem points out, this makes the task of pinning down responsibility for any disaster almost impossible – especially in the case of the *Star*, ostensibly sold by its previous owners, Sea Escape, to mysterious Danes just before it arrived in Scandinavian waters, although Harsem noticed the name Sea Escape on the key to his cabin. 'In 1992 the Danish police and prosecuting authorities took the captain of the ship and the two persons they thought were the ship-owners to court. They were charged with putting the boat into service without adequate training and without checking her safety equipment properly. They were sentenced to forty to sixty days in prison. This was appealed against and in 1993 the same persons were sentenced to the maximum sentence at that time, according to Danish law. That was six months in jail. In the event, only the captain has been to jail.

'All the time the wreck of the *Scandinavian Star* was lying in Southampton, England, and when we went to the IMO [International Maritime Organization], Torbjorn [Kalberg] and I went down to Southampton. We questioned the port authorities and others, and we found a representative from the ship-owners there. We understood that there were some questions that were not answered about who the ship-owner was.

'In February '94, the wreck was sold in London and there were just some small reports in the newspapers, but some new names were printed, International Shipping Partners, St Thomas Cruise Line. We found the people behind these companies and they tried to say they were the new ship-owners but we found out that the names were the same as those behind Sea Escape, the company that said it had sold the *Scandinavian Star* to the Danish ship-owners.'

When they started to look further they discovered more and more links that indicated that the people at Sea Escape were actually the owners of the *Star* at the time of the disaster. They concluded that the truly guilty parties had not been sent to jail. It was said that one witness, Henrik Johanssen, who was one of the ship-owners, had invested too heavily in Sea Escape to want to give evidence for fear of losing his money and because, as Harsem says, his testimony 'could ruin a much broader network of people and companies. They tried to focus on the companies in Denmark but when we found the documents on the *Scandinavian Star*, there was not one Danish address on the insurance documents in the Bahamian shipping registry. The companies were located in London and Florida, and all of them were bound to the people behind Sea Escape. We had to start a new campaign for a new investigation, but it was too late to take people to court.'

He makes the contrast between the anonymity available to ship-owners but not to car-owners. 'If the police stop me in my car I have to show them my documents, and the first thing they will look at is who is the owner of this car. If you are on an oil tanker, a bulk carrier, a passenger ferry or a cruise ship, no one asks who's the owner and that's crazy. That's the only industry where no one asks, "Who is responsible – this company or this ship or this operation?" No one asks.' Hence, a long and frustrating campaign for greater openness.

'The official version of the ownership and the responsibility for the *Scandinavian Star*,' Harsem says, 'concluded that the Danish ship-owners were the real ship-owners. The Florida- and the Bahamian-based company, Sea Escape, were the former owners, but we found out that the people connected to Sea Escape were involved in a lot of companies. It could not be true that they had just sold the ship to the new Danish ship-owners and had nothing more to do with her.'

The key name was International Shipping Partners, a new ship-owning company registered in Denmark on 1 April 1990 – 'the same day' says Harsem, 'as the *Scandinavian Star* was put on to the Norway–Denmark route. The key people include Niels Erik Lund, a former employee of the Danish company DFDS, Fred Kassner, Stuart Graff and Louis Pietro. They were never focused on in the investigation. These people have a lot of interests. Fred Kassner is involved in different travel agencies and travel-related companies. Stuart Graff works with Niels Erik Lund on investment in ships. Another person was involved in the gambling business in Florida and in the cruise industry. Louis Pietro was involved in the supply industry to these ships. But Niels Erik Lund is the brain in this system, and his way of operating ships is in the name of his company, International Shipping Partners. At every place he has some people to front these activities. Lund finds a ship and he calls his network of investors and he says to them, "Do you want to be a partner on this ship?" Someone will take one share, some another part of it. Then they create other companies in flag-of-convenience nations and they find some place in the world where they can put this ship into routes.'

The people – and the operation – are based in Florida and, incredibly, they still operate the *Scandinavian Star*. The ship, says Harsem, 'has been controlled by these people since the middle of the 1980s. Niels Erik Lund was never asked questions by the police. In 1995 they tried to put another passenger ferry, the *Beauport*, on to a route to Oslo. This ship never came to Norway but in 1996 she sailed in the Mediterranean and was rented to some people who made pornographic movies on board ship, but no one has investigated these people and put together this information, so no one has put together the complete story about International Shipping Partners and Niels Erik Lund's concept of shipping.'

Unfortunately for Harsem and his colleagues, and despite considerable newspaper publicity, their campaign has had only limited success, partly because of the lack of international action but also because of the partnership structure of the ship-owners. It's a perfect concept, says Harsem, 'because it's nearly impossible to find out where to put the responsibility. The ships are operated from Florida but the flag state is mostly the Bahamas and the ships are operated in international waters – for instance, between Norway and Denmark. We filed a complaint two years ago, against these people and their companies, to the prosecutors in Florida and in New Jersey, where Fred Kassner is located. They couldn't do anything about it because the office is located in the United States but the flag is another country and the ships are put on a route in yet another country. There is no national authority that can go into this and cut this mess of companies – I mean, just go into the core of it and make someone responsible. That's a big problem.'

The danger is now back in American waters. Unbelievably, 'The *Scandinavian Star* has been *en route* between Texas and Honduras for a while and I think it's still on a route between these countries but how should the Americans know that they are boarding the *Scandinavian Star*? The name of the ship today is *Regal Voyager*. How can they know that the ship-owner is the same ship-owner as in 1990 in the Skagerrak and in 1988 when the *Scandinavian Star* also caught fire, and the same ship-owner as in many other accidents and fires. You can look at the record of Sea Escape and International Shipping Partners.'

This is truly horrifying. 'In 1984 there was a fire on the *Scandinavian Sea*, and in 1984 on the *Scandinavian Sun*, resulting in two deaths. In 1988, the *Scandinavian Star* was on fire, in 1990 the *Scandinavian Star* again, with

158 deaths. In 1994 the *Regal Empress* caught fire outside New York with 1,400 people evacuated, and in 1995 another ship was wrecked shortly after it changed name to the *Club Royale*. But this is not the complete record.'

Professor Erichsen still mistrusts ferries. He buys 'very expensive tickets to sleep on the upper deck and I have been very heavily criticized by other members of my family because I have chosen that kind of cabin but I know what I am doing. I always sleep on the upper deck. Always.'

7

Must a Crisis Always Become a Catastrophe?

Then we heard low-flying jets above, and we even had a fishing-boat come, I'm sure, right out of Deboe Bay and right at us. We saw his lights and he came so close we could see into the windows of his boat and saw him standing there. He had his rain gear on and everything, but we had no flashlights, no flares, nothing to notify anybody that we were in the water and he just went right on by us.

'Frosty' Sloan, passenger on the *Cougar*, 15 September 1988.

The story of maritime disasters is full of examples of human frailty, stupidity or incompetence transforming what might have been a crisis into a catastrophe. Depoe Bay, described as 'the world's smallest harbour by the world's largest ocean', is a little tourist community in Oregon that used to depend on commercial fishing until charter fishing caught on. On 15 September 1988 the *Cougar*, one of the twenty-two charter fishing-boats based there, set off with six paying passengers and a crew of three for a spot of tuna fishing on what was supposed to be an eighteen-hour trip. But only five of the nine aboard survived the resulting disaster.

The *Cougar* had been built during the Second World War as a picket-boat so it was over thirty-five years old at the time of the accident. Despite its age 'the coastguard had certified the *Cougar*,' says Richard Johnson, an NTSB investigator. 'It had a certificate of inspection that allowed it to operate not more than 20 miles offshore, with not more than twenty passengers. But the coastguard also permitted vessels like the *Cougar* to operate as an uninspected vessel when carrying six or fewer passengers' – so, in theory, she could go further out.

There were warning signs on the three-and-a-half-hour outward journey: 'Frosty' Sloan, a passenger on his first trip, noticed something that seemed 'strange. The captain came down one time, slid the engine cover back and poured in another gallon of oil while it was running, without even checking it. With my background, the machinery I work with, that seemed unusual. You usually check the oil before you pour oil in. He also came down several times from where they were steering the boat to put a flashlight in between his teeth and look over the stern and underneath the boat as much as he could. This was in the dark before the sun even came up. He never said anything, but I thought he must have been checking for something, but it wasn't anything to alarm you and that's just the way the trip went.'

After some agreeable hours' fishing the captain said it was time to return. 'When he came down and told us it was time to go back,' says Frosty, 'he slid the engine cover back and poured another gallon of oil in that engine, again without checking it, and then he checked some valves that were on the wall of the cabin, water valves to the pump. They had a bilge pump underneath the boat and he would check the sides of the boat to see if any water was being pumped out. Then he would change the valve and go to another valve then check the side again. So he was checking to see if there was any water in the bottom of the boat, to see if it needed to be pumped out. And then we just headed back and there were no apparent problems at that time.'

The *Cougar* was big enough to require two properly qualified captains on board and by then Captain Pat Watson had handed over to a friend, Captain Andy Liddell, who at first had been reluctant to come on the trip. He had agreed because Watson would have lost a lot of money if he hadn't been able to go out. 'Being a nice guy, I said yes I'll go,' says Liddell, adding, 'I probably won't be such a nice guy next time, ha!'

Within an hour, he says, the *Cougar* 'felt funny, a little bit heavy on the stern, so I woke the captain up' (Frosty claims that the passengers 'hollered at him') 'and he went down on deck to check things out. When he came back he reported that water was running over the deck and he had found that the after compartment of the vessel was filled with water. So at that point I turned the vessel around into the sea and just let her idle. Went down to look the situation over myself and, yeah, there was a lot of water on deck and the stern was dropped a little bit in the water and water was flowing in through the scuppers. The relief vents are at deck height and they had flappers there. For some reason [because they had been fitted incorreclty] the flappers over the scupper would let water in, but would not let it run back off the boat and that was a real concern of mine.

'At that point I went up into the wheel-house and we took the sea cushions, tore them apart and stuffed them into the scuppers hopefully to stop water running across the deck. That seemed to work for a while and then the stern seemed to be dropping further and we couldn't figure out where the water was coming from. Did a quick check that everything seemed to be hooked up and functioning. The engine was still running. We had the bilge pump running, [but] it was not keeping up with the water coming in. I can only speculate that some planks popped loose and we were taking on water that way. Once the water level got to the height of the air intake of the engine, the engine started to splutter, the boat swung around and started taking on water over the stern quarter.'

'The first thing the captain did,' says Frosty, 'was cut up some starfoam or foam-rubber pad that he had up the stairs and told us to try to stuff it in those holes, but it wouldn't stay in, the water would just wash it right out. So we started getting buckets, trash cans, anything we could find and just started bailing water out. He turned the boat around to where the waves were hitting the bow and just kept the engine going at a slow speed and we just kept doing that and he kept trying to adjust those valves. But they still didn't show any water coming out the sides. The pump must have been either not working or it was plugged up, because the water that *was* coming out was milky in colour, like when you mix oil and water.'

As the vessel was going down they tried to send out distress signals but, as Liddell puts it, 'It seemed like Pat went into shock. Being the master of the vessel it should have been his responsibility. We did have VHF and a CB radio and I tried emergency channels first, coastguard channels for Mayday, any station, but with no reply. I tried every channel on the VHF, every channel on the CB. All indications to me on the radio were that they were transmitting with no reply.' Meanwhile they were reassuring the passengers. Frosty says, 'They said that they were going to contact the coastguard and get some pumps out here and everything would be fine, but we didn't know the radios weren't working and they couldn't get hold of the coastguard. They didn't think their signal was going out. So we just kept going until the engine died. Then we put on our life jackets.'

When they lowered themselves into the water, Frosty says, 'we still were under the assumption that the coastguard was on their way and that we were probably just going to be in the water for a short time. We didn't have any life-rafts because they weren't required. He had all the life equipment on board that he was required to have at that time. They had a couple of life-rings, great big orange oval-shaped rings, and you throw them in the water and they have ropes tied to them and you jump in the water and hang on to the ropes, and with the life jackets that was basically all we had. When the boat started to go down, we just jumped off and all got together round that life-ring and held on to those ropes.'

About an hour later the grim truth emerged. Frosty says that the captain 'finally told us that they weren't sure their radios were working. They had seen some boats during the day and had tried to make contact with them to find out how the fishing was and they couldn't contact boats they could see. So here we were, 35 miles from shore, and they didn't think there was any chance they'd contacted the coastguard. They were just hoping that maybe somebody had heard their signals and that they would contact the coast-guard and that they would be out to get us. Things didn't look too good, because we'd already been in the water for an hour and I'd always heard that if you're in water off the Oregon coast without any survival equipment you don't last more than a couple or three hours. It was starting to get dark, so I just didn't think there was much chance that we were going to survive at all.'

The master of the vessel was the first to succumb to hypothermia. 'I think,' says Andy Liddell, 'it was due to shock, seeing his vessel go down and it all being his responsibility. So there we were. The passengers didn't know what to do. I've had lots of cold-water training and survival, and at the time I was going through an EMT class, as an emergency medical tech-nician. In my training I learned that in cold water you lose most of your heat from your armpits, your head and your groin and by using energy, so I told these people to stay still, not to move or talk, and stay huddled up. During the night, two people perished and as they did, whatever line was left over from tying the two flotation devices together we tied the dead bodies to that and everybody stayed together. So when we were rescued everybody came home, but not everybody was alive.

'Sometimes I saw search planes up above. It was a nice clear night, I could see the stars, the ocean wasn't rough but in going from boat to water the night flares had disappeared. I don't know where they went, they must have fallen out of my jacket. One of the passengers asked me to light the day flares and I couldn't do that. They're not designed to work at night, they're just smoke, they don't glow. We spent a very long night out there.'

Frosty takes up the story. 'During the night we heard a jet fly over and a helicopter. You could tell that they were working a search pattern, because they would go over and then disappear.

'Then we heard low-flying jets above, and we even had a fishing-boat come, I'm sure, right out of Depoe Bay and right at us. We saw his lights and he came so close we could see into the windows of his boat and saw him standing there. He had his rain gear on and everything, but we had no flash-lights, no flares, nothing to notify anybody that we were in the water and he just went right on by us.'

'Generally,' says Liddell, 'a search isn't started unless a vessel is missing for over twenty-four hours. I was due at a meeting in Depoe Bay that night at seven o'clock. I'm pretty prompt. At eight or nine o'clock no word had been heard from us and it was unlike me not to be there or having communication, so the charter office we ran out of had contacted the coastguard, told them the situation and they started the search – thankfully, otherwise none of us might be here today.' Nevertheless the helicopters did not spot them until nearly 11 a.m. the next day, a full eighteen hours after they had abandoned ship.

The worst moment came just before they were rescued. Liddell says, 'The last person to perish from hypothermia was Rick Moore, the deckhand on the vessel. He looked at me and said, "Andy, I can't take it here any longer, I'm swimming home." He untied himself and swam away. Neither I nor anybody else could go after him because that would have been exert-ing energy and we might have had more deaths. He didn't make it. Fifty yards away and he was face down. Within minutes of that the helicopter flew over and when it hovered above us, I signalled to it to go get that guy. I think Rick could have been saved. It was a cold-water drowning, in my opinion, and I think if they had picked him up first he could have survived, but they flew over, they hovered, they assessed the situation and what they saw was what looked like a dead body, so they came to where we were.'

Fortunately for the investigators, they recovered a camera. It had belonged to the only female passenger, Cally Wynne, who did not survive the accident. 'This camera and the film inside of it was taken and developed,' says Richard Johnson, 'and although we did not believe at the time that the film would come out, because it had been immersed in salt-water for a long time, the pictures were very clear. They provided us with a great deal of information about the condition of the *Cougar* prior to the incident. The most important aspect of the pictures was the fact that water was washing across the after-deck of this vessel during the early morning, when everybody was engaged in fishing. It shows that nobody seemed concerned about it. It also shows us certain physical characteristics of the *Cougar*, specifically how the hatch-covers were constructed. These photographs gave us definitive information indicating that the hatch-covers were not watertight and, in fact, were not designed to be. They also gave us information about the freeing ports [holes which allow water to flow out, but not in], specifically that the flaps on them were fitted on the inboard side. As a result the water was seeping in through the freeing ports and then, as the vessel rolled, the water started flowing back towards the freeing port, and the flap would close, trapping that water on board. Normally if the flaps are on the outboard side, the water would drain out and the pressure of the sea would close that flap, preventing more water from coming on board.' The photographs 'nailed down how this significant amount of flooding could have gotten ahead of them.

'Another feature that these photographs showed was the modifications made to the vessel over the years. This whole wheel-house was added and quite a number of changes were made to the boat, which increased its draught. With the addition of some fuel tanks and a sewage tank, the vessel was riding lower in the water than it was originally designed to do. We found out later that between the engine compartment and the lazarette [separate bulkheaded compartment] there was originally a void space, but during some modification to the vessel years earlier they had put these additional fuel tanks in there, which interrupted the watertight integrity between the lazarette and the void space, so you created a huge area for water to collect. And the pumps on this vessel were not designed to handle that kind of flooding.'

Even the experts can sometimes get it wrong. In January 1991 the fishing-boat *Sea King* sank at the mouth of the Columbia river off the coast of Washington. The trouble started when a member of the crew was sent into the hold to stop flooding in the lazarette. According to NTSB investigator Richard Johnson, 'It was their plan to drain the lazarette into the engine compartment. What happened, however, was that the deckhand, in clearing the drain, took this flexible hose off and didn't refasten it. Instead of the water going directly into the engine compartment, it went into the after part of the fish hold. Eventually it went forward and started seeping into the engine compartment because the bulkhead between the engine compartment and the fish hold was not watertight. And that's when they started noticing water and started de-watering the engine compartment.'

At about 8.40 a.m., when they realized they couldn't pump out the water, they called the coastguard. Richard Johnson tells the story: 'The coastguard sent out a helicopter with a number of pumps, which they lowered to the *Sea King*. The crew had trouble starting these pumps, so the coastguards also lowered one of the rescue swimmers from the helicopter, who was trained in the operation of the pumps, to help get them going. They had a number of problems with the pumps, and that continued through most of the day.

'A four-motor lifeboat from the National Motor Lifeboat School at Cape Disappointment was in the vicinity of the Columbia river bar in a training exercise, so it was dispatched to see what assistance it could provide. Over a period of time the coastguards put four people on board the *Sea King*, to help in the de-watering. What we found was that much of the information about the efforts made by the operator to contain the flooding on board his vessel was not communicated to the coastguards, so when they came on board they didn't have a clear idea of what the problem was flooding-wise. All they knew was that there was flooding in the engine compartment. They didn't realize that there was also flooding in the fish hold, or that it had originated in the lazarette. So most of the efforts made were to de-water the engine compartment, and this caused problems later on.'

Initially, says Johnson, 'They lowered the rescue swimmer from the helicopter, and he was having problems with the pumps, so the helicopter went back and got two more people. The plan was to drop these two additional people on board the *Sea King* to help them with the pumps, and to take off two crew members. The first was hoisted safely from the *Sea King*, but during the hoisting of the second the cable got caught in the *Sea King*'s rigging and broke, dropping this individual on to the after-deck of the *Sea King*.'

According to Johnson, the coastguards noticed later that many of the bolts on the cover of the hatch to the fish hold were missing. 'We think,' says Johnson, 'that although this was not the source of the original flooding, it certainly exacerbated the situation. It made it even more difficult for their pumps to keep up.' Nevertheless, at one point it was believed that with the engine compartment dry they could make an attempt to cross the bar. But the *Sea King* had problems with its fuel filters too: the engine kept stalling and the sea conditions were such that they aborted the first attempt. Johnson goes on: 'While the efforts were under way to pump out the engine compartment, there was a discussion going on as to whether or not to make an attempt to cross the bar. About eleven thirty that morning the decision

Three – imaginary – views of the sinking of the *Titanic*. All are drawings from *The Illustrated London News*. The centre drawing has a number of superimposed quotes, ranging from 'The starlight [sic] night was beautiful' to 'Every porthole and saloon was blazing with light.'

Above: The biggest spill of them all – the *Amoco Cadiz* goes down off Brittany on 16 March 1978, spilling 223,000 tons of oil.

Below*:* A recent horror: the bulk carrier *Flare* sinks after breaking in two off the coast of Newfoundland in January 1998 with a loss of twenty-one of the twenty-five members of the crew.

Above: An image of beauty – and horror: the ferry *Scandinavian Star* as she is brought into port after fire broke out on 7 September 1990 killing 158 people while she was on a voyage from Norway to Denmark.

Below: Deceptively peaceful: the apparently limited damage on board the *Scandinavian Star* concealed the bodies of the men, women and children suffocated by poisonous fumes as they struggled to escape from their cabins below deck.

Above: The most extraordinary rescue of them all: the upturned hull of the yacht *Exide Challenger* after it had capsized in the southern Indian Ocean during a Round the World Race in 1996. The yachtsman, Tony Bullimore, survived for six days before being rescued by the Australian navy.

Opposite: The bow door of the ro-ro ferry *Estonia* which sank in the icy waters of the Baltic on 18 November 1004, killing 852 of those aboard from drowning – or hypothermia. It subsequently emerged that the ship suffered from an appalling lack of maintenance.

Below: A search and rescue team from the Philippine navy saves survivors from the *Cebu City*, one of the many over-crowded passenger ferries which sink every year in the waters between the 7,000 islands of the Philippine Archipelago.

Above: The biggest clean-up of all. Removing oil from some of the hundreds of miles of the Alaskan shore-line after the *Exxon Valdez* had run aground in Prince WIlliam Sound just after midnight on 24 March 1989.

Below left: 'Operation Teaspoon', the aptly named exercise in removing the oil from the beaches of Brittany after the *Amoco Cadiz* had run aground.

Below right: Oil on the rocks. In January 1993 the oil tanker *Braer* ran aground in the Shetlands. Fortunately the waves which had driven her on to the rocks dispersed the oil without causing too much pollution.

Two views of the biggest British disaster in peacetime since the *Titanic*, the sinking of the *Herald of Free Enterprise* just off the Belgian port of Zeebrugge on 6 March 1987. Even though rescue vessels arrived within minutes and the crew performed heroically, 193 of the near-600 passengers and crew were drowned because the ship sank so quickly after water had entered the car deck.

Above: The end of the *Achille Lauro*, unluckiest of cruise liners, after she had caught fire in 1994, killing three of those on board. She had already been ravaged by fire in 1982. Three years later an elderly American passenger was killed after the liner was hijacked by Palestinian guerrillas.

Below: The most amazing incident of all. On 6 January 1987 the freighter *Bright Field* crashed into a hotel and shopping centre after she had lost engine power while trying to dock in New Orleans.

BRIGHT FIELD

was made to use a much larger lifeboat, the *Triumph*, to tow the *Sea King* because the fishing-boat's engine kept stalling. Unfortunately they didn't get very far. They were probably about forty minutes into the crossing when some breaking seas on the bar literally laid one of the motor lifeboats on its side and they turned around. There was an ebb current running in the river and this exacerbates bar conditions. They had to head back out to sea.

'The discussion now turned on whether or not to take the injured person off the *Sea King*.' He refused to go. 'As the vessel moved offshore after the first attempt to cross the bar, things stabilized. They moved further offshore into deeper water, sea conditions moderated, and they were able to get a handle on the flooding in the engine compartment. The conditions improved so much that consideration was given to making a second attempt, but not until after the tide had turned. So in the interim, in order to give the crew on the motor lifeboats an opportunity to get some rest, they sent the other boats back to Station Cape Disappointment. One boat was left on the scene. During the late afternoon they also made the decision to dispatch the coastguard cutter *Iris* to help, with the idea that it was a bigger platform from which to monitor the entire operation.'

Once the *Iris* arrived they decided to return to port. According to Jeff Rusiecki, the the coxwain of the first lifeboat on the scene, 'We'd probably been towing for three or four hours right up to the time that the boat suddenly rolled and sank. There was no indication up until that time that anything was going to go wrong. In fact, I think the feeling was just the opposite, that we had gotten this one done successfully and in a couple of hours we would be back at the station and warm.'

The only sign of possible trouble came when the master of the *Sea King* told Rusiecki that 'he was going to increase his speed a little bit. I had a little concern then that he might overtake the tow line and warned him against that. I brought my speed up to match his. I believe that was the last conversation I had with him, which was several minutes before the boat sank. It sounded like everything was fine, the pumps were secured and it looked like it would be a normal crossing for that time of year.'

Unfortunately they had grossly underestimated the problems of trying to tow a boat in the conditions prevailing where the Columbia river reaches the sea. As David Fasterbend, who was responsible for piloting the boat over the sand bars at the mouth of the river, explains: 'The Columbia river's got a tidal change in the winter time, sometimes up to twelve feet, maybe a little more. The current generated from that tide change will reach upwards to five to six knots. When it comes out of the estuary and reaches the Pacific Ocean, which is driven in from a westerly wind, you have a large westerly swell coming in here meeting a westerly driven current coming from the river. It creates large, peaked, breaking waves and they are hard to navigate. It makes for just a miserable stretch of water.'

As might be expected, Johnson sees the final débâcle somewhat differently. 'The vessel at one point started to assume a port list and the person at the helm of the *Sea King* said, "Hey, we're starting to go over here, we're abandoning ship". And that was basically the last transmission and everybody was scattering to get off. And then she rolled over fairly quickly.' Three of the seven people on board – two of the crew and a coastguardsman – drowned.

'Basically there were three factors affecting the *Sea King* just before the capsize. You have the weight of the water in the lazarette, the fish hold and the engine compartment. In addition to that, you have several tons of ice, like four tons of ice, several tons of fish, and you have fuel that was on board the vessel. So you have the weight of the water. Now you have the effect of free surface, which is reducing the vessel's stability, and on top of that you have the movement of the sea. So all these factors, you know, are happening at the same time. And, really, it only was a matter of time before one or two or three of these factors got in synch with one another and things deteriorated quickly. That's what we believe happened.

'Really what this accident boils down to is that when you have a search-and-rescue incident, and the coastguards are being asked to come and help a vessel, it's absolutely critical for the crew aboard to provide the coast-guards with all the information they have about the nature of the emergency. The coastguards are coming on board the vessel with their rigs, pumps, personnel, and bring their boats, helicopters, and they know there's some flooding maybe, but they're not sure where. So it's incumbent upon the crew of the boat to provide *all* information to the coastguard relating to the nature of their emergency. It is also incumbent upon the coastguard to make sure this information's given to them. And that's one of the things that we believe could have helped this situation.'

Rusiecki still doesn't know how things went so wrong: 'I just couldn't put my finger on it. There were a lot of people out there who were doing everything they could do to save that boat and that crew and it was a shock when we turned around and saw it going over.'

8
Ole Man Killer

We've never had a ship that's hit a hotel before.
                              Marjorie Murtagh, NTSB investigator

Major maritime disasters are not confined to the open seas, or to crowded channels like those in the Philippines. Probably the most crowded and dangerous sea passage in the world is the Bosphorus, which separates Europe from Asia. To the inhabitants of Istanbul, which spans the straits, the inevitable collisions are sometimes seen as a spectator sport, as in Orhan Panuk's childhood reminiscences:* 'Do I remember, they say, the time when an excursion boat sank somewhere between Yenikoy and Beykoz with the members of the Turkish-German Association on board? Or that time when a Romanian tanker called *Ploesti* just barely touched a fishing-boat and, in the blink of an eye, the fishing-boat went down in two pieces?' Then there was the boat that went down with 20,000 sheep on board: 'A few of the sheep managed to jump ship and swim ashore, where they were rescued by Istanbulites who a minute before had been reading their newspapers in tea-houses along the Bosphorus; the rest of the hapless creatures are still waiting for their rescuers at the bottom of the sea.'

But at times the collisions brought danger to the watching locals on the banks of the Bosphorus. When a Greek and a Yugoslav tanker collided, the oil caught fire,

> with an explosion that was heard all over Istanbul. The crews on
> both the tankers had instantly burned to death even as they tried
> abandoning ship; without anyone at the helm, both vessels were
> running around out of control, dragged every which way by the
> heavy and unfathomable currents and whirlpools of the Bosphorus,

The Boy Who Watched the Ships Go By, Granta 61, The Sea, London, 1998.

bursting into fireballs that threatened the suburbs on both shores. People abandoned their homes and, carrying their quilts and children, tried to get away from the sea. The Yugoslavian tanker drifted to the European side and slammed into the passenger ship *Tarsus*, which soon caught fire. The sea was ablaze and the water looked intensely yellow. The ships had turned into infernal masses of metal; the funnels, the masts, the captain's bridges had melted and collapsed. The sea was lit by a red light that seemed to come from the bowels of the ships. Explosions went off at intervals, and shards of sheet iron the size of blankets fell into the sea like burning sheets of paper; screams and cries rose up from the hills and the beaches; the loud crying of babies could be heard after each eruption.

Occasionally a wreck actually penetrated the lives and houses of those on shore. In 1963 a Russian freighter went aground on the banks of the Bosphorus, destroying two houses and killing three of the inhabitants. 'The papers printed a photograph of the freighter wedged into the living room. The snout of the ship had pushed its way into familiar furniture, the same kind of chairs, tables, sofas, we had in our homes.'

But, then, any crowded waterway brings its own problems. Three hundred ships a day pass through the Strait of Dover, providing perfect conditions for collision, not only between ships going in opposite directions but between ships passing through the Strait and the ferries steaming across their path on their way between France and Britain. Surprisingly, perhaps, there are only four collisions on average per year. Although there are separate channels for ships travelling in different directions, says Eric Musson, coastguards' operations manager at Dover, 'at the moment there is only compulsory reporting for vessels carrying dangerous cargo – that's oils, chemicals, gas, explosives, anything like that. For other ships at the moment it is voluntary and we only know the names of about twenty-five per cent of the ships that pass through. But, at this time, there are representations being made to the International Maritime Organization that, together with France, we will declare the Dover Strait a compulsory reporting area for all vessels over 300 gross tons.' Until then, if a ship doesn't report, 'Well, we track it but we're tracking an unknown target. We can't tell from the radar display what type of ship is being tracked unless it speaks to us.'

Fishing-vessels are the greatest problem, 'because,' says Musson, 'by the very nature of their job, they obstruct the lane, and other ships have difficulty in keeping in the lanes and avoiding the fishing-vessels. They can fish in the separation zones quite happily without causing any trouble to anybody but, of course, sometimes they want to fish in the traffic lanes themselves and there they should fish in the direction of the traffic flow and not impede the passage of a vessel following the lane. But if we get a concentration of fishing-vessels in the traffic lanes they can cause an obstruction and this is probably the biggest problem in the Dover Strait traffic-separation scheme.'

Unfortunately, if the coastguards see a concentration that's causing a traffic problem they 'can't do anything about it because we don't control the shipping in the Strait as air-traffic control controls aircraft. There is freedom of navigation for vessels of all nations and it is up to the master of each vessel to navigate his vessel according to international rules. We observe and report, and our report may be in the form of a broadcast warning to other ships of a concentration of fishing-vessels.'

The potential for a collision between a fishing-boat and one of the other users of the Strait was realized on the night of 10–11 August 1991 with the sinking of the fishing-boat *Ocean Hound*. At about 5 a.m. on the eleventh, says Musson, 'an emergency indicator beacon was picked up by satellite and we were informed of its position. We then concentrated a search in that position for the *Ocean Hound* but all we found was the buoy, a bit of wreckage and one body. It then transpired that this vessel had called us earlier on, and said that she was going to cross the south-west lane and go down towards Dungeness to fish.' When they replayed the radar videotape they found that 'the trawler didn't do what she said she was going to do. In fact she turned back into the south-west lane and started fishing. It was thick fog when she did this and another ship, or ships, passed so close to her that it seems that she was either struck or capsized by the close proximity of the other ships. She was probably struck by another ship who had no idea that she had touched her – but it was sufficient to cause some damage to her bottom and turn her upright. As she sank the beacon was released and started transmitting.'

The tragedy remained a mystery. 'How,' asks Musson, 'if the *Ocean Hound* had crossed the lane and turned back into it, was the beacon activated some way to the north? It was believed that the vessel was struck or capsized in this stretch of water and drifted along. At some point later it was struck by another ship, which wouldn't have known anything about it; it turned upright and sank and then the beacon was activated. The beacon couldn't be activated in the first instance because the vessel was upside down and it was only when the vessel came upright that the beacon could be released. This has now been addressed and beacons are in such a position on vessels that they can be released whether the vessel's upside down or not.'

The example of the *Ocean Hound* illustrates the dilemma posed by fishing-boats in so crowded a stretch of water. 'Fishing-vessels are reluctant to tell anybody where they're fishing because their report is made over an open radio channel which all their colleagues can hear. They'll know then exactly where they're fishing and where the best fishing area is at that time. Often a fishing-vessel is overdue at its port and we don't know where to start looking because we don't know where they're fishing and yet the *Ocean Hound* this time, most unusually, called Dover coastguard before she crossed the south-west lane. And that is what we wish to encourage but, unfortunately, she didn't do what she said she was going to do. One of the most important lessons to be learned from this tragic incident is that if fishing-vessels were to report their position more frequently, then there'd always be a better chance of being able to deal with any trouble they might get into.' The coastguard could also 'warn them of weather conditions that are coming up. Another problem in the Dover Strait is fog banks. When the *Ocean Hound* called us she said she'd got three miles visibility, but half an hour later, when she started fishing, the visibility in her area was barely half a mile.' As is so often the case 'the technology is already available. The fishing-vessels should be fitted with a transponder, so that they can be automatically identified in a particular position and nobody else need know except the shore station receiving the automatic identification.'

As it was, neither the coastguard nor the lawyers representing various interests were able to establish the name of the vessel that passed close to or contacted the *Ocean Hound*. 'Of course,' says Musson, 'if they'd been fitted with transponders [electronic device identifying a particular ship] then their identity would never have been in doubt.' But they were able to plot the drift of the *Ocean Hound* to where the beacon was found: the radar record 'suggests that she must have come across a nice shoal of fish as she crossed the lane and changed her mind over the plans she told us earlier'.

Every narrow channel or large river has its own tale of woe to tell. In 1986 the Egyptian luxury tourist ship *Nubia* – with twenty-eight cabins, and equipped with a solarium and a swimming-pool – capsized and sank in the Nile between Aswan and Luxor because a sandstorm had caused freak currents in the river. Thirty-one lives were lost although sixty-eight people survived.

In August 1989 the British public was horrified when fifty-one young people, at a party on the river steamer *Marchioness*, were drowned on the river Thames in central London. Not only was this by far the worst recorded disaster in modern times on the river, it also featured the oldest vessel involved in an accident in modern times: the *Marchioness* dated back to 1923. It collided with a motor dredger, the *Bowbelle*, which ripped off the *Marchioness*'s upper deck. The *Bowbelle* survived and changed its name several times before eventually it broke in two and sank off the coast of Madeira seven years later.

Of all the narrow waters, the most dangerous has to be the lower reaches of the mighty Mississippi, with its fatal combination of shallow, swirling, treacherous waters, incompetent pilots and overcrowding. Many pilots are not qualified but are employed thanks to their local connections. Marjorie Murtagh, an investigator from the NTSB, explains that 'The port of New Orleans is the second busiest port, I believe, in the world. About six thousand ocean-going ships and a hundred and twenty thousand tows and barges transit the Mississippi every year. The city of New Orleans is located at a right-angle bend in the river. It's called Algiers Point, and it's a 90-degree turn that these ships have to make when they're either down-bound or up-bound.'

The most spectacular recent result of the overcrowding came shortly after 2 p.m. on 14 December 1996 when the fully loaded Liberian-registered bulk carrier *Bright Field* temporarily lost power as she was navigating outbound on the lower Mississippi at New Orleans. The vessel struck a wharf near a commercial section of the city, which included a shopping mall, the garage for a condominium and a hotel. No one was killed and no one aboard the ship was hurt, but sixty-two people were injured, four seriously, while shore facilities, a gaming vessel and an excursion boat moored nearby were evacuated. Fortunately the ship had not collided with any of the other vessels but, even so, the damage amounted to over $20 million.

'When this accident occurred,' says Murtagh, 'the river was at high water, which meant that the speed of the water was higher than normal and therefore when the ship was operating at full speed she was transiting at an extremely rapid rate down the river.' It was clear that, contrary to the pilot's opinion, the high speed was not necessary. As it was, 'There was less than two minutes for the bridge crew to respond to the loss of power. If this had occurred out in the ocean, it would have been temporary because it was only a two-minute loss of power and it would not have had necessarily the same type of results that it did in the port of New Orleans.'

When Murtagh arrived on the scene soon after the collision, she found 'the ship herself tied up to the pier, right in front of the hotel. They were concerned about the hotel collapsing so they couldn't move the ship. When we arrived and we first went aboard the ship, it was just an incredible sight. The ship had run down the dock and had essentially wiped out the equivalent of forty hotel rooms. Mattresses were hanging out of the rooms, the venetian blinds from the windows were draped across the bow of the vessel. There was rubble everywhere. Cars had been crushed in the concrete that had come down on the parking lot. My personal response was that it was a miracle that nobody had been killed. It was only seventy feet from the *Queen of New Orleans* when it came to its final resting place. It was quite a scene, very unusual. We've never had a ship hit a hotel before.'

A maze of problems emerged during her investigations. The single most obvious was that of communication. At several key moments before and during the emergency, the pilot, the master and the crew did not communicate effectively. During her first, informal interviews, Murtagh found that 'For the people on the bridge the sequence of events was completely different than the sequence of events in the engine room, because on the bridge they could see what was occurring when the engine lost power. Whereas in the engine room, they knew that the main engine had gone off line, but they were not aware that they were so close to both the bridge and the hotel area.'

Language problems increased the chaos. 'When the accident sequence occurred, with the loss of power, the Chinese crew reverted back to Chinese, and the pilot, although his initial query was, "What's happening?", didn't pursue that any further. In the meantime he was under the impression that the Chinese crew was not doing anything to restore power, when in fact they were doing quite a bit to restore power. The conversations that were taking place in Chinese he couldn't understand.

'At the same time, the pilot had ordered the anchor dropped, and the master then tried to notify the anchor watch, who happened to be the carpenter up on the bow, to drop the anchor. Well the pilot, concerned about hitting the ships that were docked alongside, started blowing the whistle, and didn't realize that in the constant blowing of that whistle, the orders to the carpenter to drop the anchor couldn't be heard. So the carpenter never did drop the anchor. At some point during that sequence of events, the master decided to tell the carpenter not to drop the anchor anyway, because he was concerned that if he had it could very well have caused the ship to hit one of the vessels, rather than clear it completely.

'The other aspect of communication we discovered was that in the initial pilot–master exchange prior to departing the berth, the two of them hadn't talked very well. They hadn't really exchanged the necessary information for both to understand that as they passed through the city of New Orleans that would be the most critical area where there are a lot of passenger vessels and a hotel in place.'

Looking deeper into the collision, the NTSB's investigators found evidence of recurring engineering problems due to lack of adequate testing and maintenance. The ship's maintenance records showed 'that there had been long-term maintenance problems with the *Bright Field* engine room' in a situation where ships have to be operating with 100 per cent efficiency. 'Ships in very tight quarters, which is essentially the way they're working on the Mississippi river, have to be extremely manoeuvrable, because of the rapid changes in current and direction that occur. If they lose power, even for short periods of time, as the *Bright Field* did just with the two-minute sequence, it presents a potential problem that it will in fact hit a bridge. It could very well have hit the bridge as well as hitting the hotel, all of which could have had devastating results to people who were on shore.'

This is not merely a theoretical threat. 'According to coastguard data,' says Murtagh, 'there is a ship with partial loss of power at least once a week. There is a ship with total loss of power about once or twice a month. And that got us to look a bit further at exactly what aspects of this port made it perhaps particularly vulnerable to a ship losing power. We analysed all of the ships that had hit various sections of the piers within the city of New Orleans and there were about 166 down-bound collisions with the pier over the period that we looked at. We then asked the authorities what they had done to protect themselves from this particular problem, since there seemed to be a large number of ships losing power and potentially out of control that could hit not just the hotel but the cruise ships and the gambling vessels that are normally tied up to the pier. And we felt that there had not been enough done by either the coastguard or the city to protect the people aboard the passenger vessels.'

The problems of the Mississippi, the pressure of traffic, the inadequate regulatory framework, and the lack of skill among some of the pilots, were never better illustrated than in the extraordinary and tragic case of the *Mauvilla*. On 22 September 1993 this towboat was pushing a number of cargo barges up the Mobile river, a tributary of the Mississippi, in Alabama. There was heavy fog and the pilot made a wrong turn, taking his boat and the barges up another creek. At about the same time Amtrak's Los Angeles–Miami express was pulling out of Mobile station with 202 passengers on board. By the time the fog had lifted, forty-two of the passengers and five members of the train's crew had died, the majority drowned.

When the fog had come down, the pilot of the *Mauvilla* had started looking for a place to tie up. On the boat's radar screen he spotted what he thought was another towboat with its barges strung out across the river. He decided to moor up against it and wait for the fog to lift. But the shapes he had seen on his radar screen were not barges but the pontoons of the Big Bayou Canot railway bridge. 'When the *Mauvilla* came up here in the fog,' says Dave Adcock, the first coastguard on the scene, 'of course he couldn't see the banks, he couldn't see the head of the tow even. It was very thick fog at that time. However, it was quite clear on the radar, if he could interpret it. That was the problem, he really didn't know what he had on the radar because he didn't know what speed he was making. He was moving ahead, looking for somewhere to tie up his freight along the river, then wait for the fog to lift. The towboat people have favourite places they can tie up around here and he was looking for a tree or something to put a line on,' Adcock continues. In the end by heading for the 'barges' right at that moment, he misinterpreted the radar and went up the Bayou Canot rather than straight up the river, unaware of where he had turned. 'He just went too far up the wrong river. He wasn't paying attention, I guess, to where he was going.'

At the same moment the express train was approaching the same bridge at over 70 m.p.h. having been given the all-clear at Bayou Sara. The train engineer had just called the conductor to thank him for bringing him coffee while the train had stopped at Mobile station. It was to be the last cup of coffee he would ever drink. The pilot of the *Mauvilla* later testified that he had heard a 'swishing sound' and saw a fire just ahead of his boat. Believing that he was still on the Mobile river he radioed to the Mobile river bridge tender asking whether anyone had reported a fire. No one had. The assistant conductor of the express radioed a Mayday appeal. He had walked along the train and found that the whole middle section was missing. The double-decker carriages were in the river. The engine, with its driver and engineer, had buried itself in 46 feet of mud.

Brad Dicks, who was travelling on the train with his wife and his mother, woke up to find that 'The train car was shaking violently and we couldn't see outside the windows. It was pitch black. For a minute, we didn't know what was going on, but soon we realized that the train had to be wrecking. It started leaning to one side and you could hear timbers cracking and breaking. When it finally came to rest we realized that it had stopped and we were all in one piece, but we didn't know where we were. The train began to sink and water began to rush in the top floor of the car, but I was able to get out of the window with my wife and my mother because we knew where the emergency exit was.

'When we surfaced up to the top of the water, we were very disoriented – you could see the flames shooting up from the rest of the train.' His wife Susannah remembers how, when they were in the water, 'The fire was so hot that it was burning our faces. We weren't really close to it, but it felt like we were and we knew we had to get as far away from the fire as we could, so we began to swim toward the bridge and we got to it. That's all I really remember about it.'

'Everything was pitch black,' says Brad, 'so we were unable to see where the bank was. We didn't know how wide the river was or anything. Off to the distance we could see a spotlight but we didn't know what it was coming from, but we managed to get hold of a cross tie that was floating in the water and worked our way back to the portion of the bridge that was left and just hung on there for a while. Finally some people from the train came down to the edge of the water and shone a flashlight and we were able to make it back to the shore.'

It was far more difficult for his wife: 'We were beginning to float away and the film of diesel was really strong on top of the water. It was hard to breathe and all that was sticking out the water was your head. We could hear other people trying to get help and then we were floating away. We knew we had to get back. So we swam back toward the bridge – we knew it had to lead to the land. I remember getting out and looking back but I never looked back again after that.'

Once he'd done his checks and retired to sleep, John Turk, the chief train conductor, happened to think back 'to when I was first hired and the gentleman who trained me had told me that the best way to sleep on a train was with your feet facing forward. I thought it was odd to think back almost twenty years on something that I was taught, but it turned out to be very useful. That night I did set up my bedding with my feet facing forward.' A couple of hours later he was woken by a violent shock that he knew from experience had been caused by a derailment. At that point no one knew how bad the accident was, 'but each car as I went seemed to reveal how bad it really was. First I came upon the dining car, and it was a shock just to see everything in complete disarray throughout the car. It almost seemed like a hurricane had been through it.'

Further forward he could see flames. In the lower compartments of the two-level section of the train 'there's what we call a handicap section for those passengers who are physically challenged. There were three passengers I realized were trapped inside this section, because the door would not open. I tried to open the door by using a key, using the press button that automatically opens it. Neither of these things responded. I tried to pull the door open, that wouldn't work either, so at that point I took a sledgehammer from the emergency kit, knocked the little plastic window in, and got the passengers out.'

Only when he went towards the front end of the car did he realize that 'We were on a bridge and the bridge was gone. There were cars in the water, there were flames apparently coming from the engine and the crew-car section. I went back towards the rear of the train, exited by the last car, dialled 911 on the mobile phone and asked the conductor for our location. Unfortunately, at that time of night, in the fog, with the unexpectedness of the accident, he himself wasn't sure where we were, so I gave the only information he could give me. He believed we were in the Mobile river.

'Then I went back on board with the other employees. We began gathering blankets, pillows, whatever we could get, first-aid kits, emergency lights, flashlights. Then we thought about flotation devices for the people in the water. We came back outside, opened up the emergency windows, and were throwing all of these things out of the windows. We noticed that there was a tugboat over to my right. I tried to use this flashlight to signal the pilot toward the accident and toward where we were. I guess the first thing I thought about was, My gosh, I hope these people aren't going to be eaten by alligators.'

At the time the general feeling among everyone was one of shock. Finally, a rescue train was backed down to the site and the professionals took over. Only then did Turk discover how many friends and colleagues he had lost. 'I finally called my family, talked to my wife and the tears didn't come until, oh, gosh, I guess almost . . . eighteen hours after the accident occurred.'

Fortunately for the rescue operation the operations officer for the local coastguard and the watch-stander for the Marine Safety Office were together, as they were most nights (being a married couple): Randy and Debroah Scott. 'I guess a little after three in the morning,' says Debroah, 'I got a call from a bridge-tender who was very excited. He was saying, "There's people in the water, we've had a train wreck, there's fire". He had a real thick accent and I had just woken up and I could not understand. I said, "OK, where are you talking about?" And he said, "Bayou Sailboat." Well, there's no Bayou Sailboat that I could think of but sometimes there's local names. I said, "On the Mobile river?" Yeah, yeah. "Well where is it in reference to Three Mile Creek?" And that's when he gave me, "Oh, about two and a half miles." And since he gave me a name which I thought was bogus I thought it was a hoax. Like, I almost forgot to get his name. And then I hung up the phone and told my husband that I was going to dispatch one of his boats because I thought we had a hoax. I handled oil spills, commercial traffic, but any time we got search-and-rescue type things I passed it over to the operations centre, so that was normal. Then we got a call from CSX Railroad and that's when I knew it wasn't a hoax, because they said, yes, we've had a train in the water.'

'Before she even had a chance to hang up with him,' says Randy, 'I was on the other phone to my watch-stander. And, talking to him, it looked like we'd got a train derailed. Now at that time we thought it was a freight train. Nobody could place a passenger train going through Mobile, Alabama, at three o'clock in the morning. By a quarter to four I was on my way into the operations centre and on the way I realized that it was the *Sunset Limited* that had just recently started running through Mobile. We probably had a lot of people in the water. We got more helicopters to head in that direction and launched another boat or two.'

'We had been doing some drills and other planning,' says Debroah, 'so I was familiar with some of the other emergency-management people. I started to call people that I thought might be able to find the dive teams something that would make a platform for landing. We found out there were some barges in the area, some local fishermen.'

'Scott Paper had a couple of barges and tugboats that were working the river moving logs,' says Randy, 'and one of the tugboats called in and he had worked with us on an emergency-management drill we had done the summer before. He had a very large barge attached at the time and they were already moving up-river.'

'Things moved really quickly,' says Debroah. 'I'd say within about twenty-five minutes we had some radio frequencies set up and emergency-management people had established a little command under the bridge.'

By the time Debroah and Randy arrived on the scene 'there were already probably three or four tugboats either *en route* or on the scene trying to help,' says Randy. 'They noticed that one particular tugboat had a bunch of barges that had broken loose and a couple of the boats were busy trying to round them up.'

It was only when they started reviewing the audiotapes that recorded all the traffic 'that we noticed there was a tug, the *Mauvilla*, that had claimed he was having some problems. He thought he'd gotten hung up on a sand bar. And he was talking to another tugboat and he said, "Oh, looks like I got off." And when we went back later and pieced out exactly what time it would have been when he got hung up, it was probably when he hit the bridge in the fog and just didn't know it.' The pilot detached his barges and started an heroic rescue effort pulling survivors from the freezing water, still believing that he was dealing with a rail crash on the Mobile river and not that he was responsible for the derailment.

When Captain Paul Esbensen, the investigator from the NTSB, arrived on the scene the next day, 'The first thing I saw was half of the passenger car hanging off the end of the piece of bridge that was still standing. The rest of the bridge was gone. The passenger cars were in the water. I saw the tops of them but not the engines. They were firmly down in the mud. As we came up the river I noticed there was some damage to the concrete part of the bridge pier and that led to my suspicion that perhaps one of the barges had struck it. We found damage to a barge where the bridge concrete had left a good imprint on its bow.'

The pilot of the *Mauvilla*, still unaware of what had happened, was arrested, still believing, however, that he was just a rescuer rather than the cause of the collision. He was later released. He told Esbensen that he remembered a 'slight bump' while he was looking for a mooring spot in the fog but had assumed that he had run aground. In fact, of course, the towboat had hit the Big Bayou Canot railway bridge and knocked the rails out of line. Ironically, had the towboat been travelling faster and the collision been harder, the forty-seven passengers and crew might not have died. A stronger impact might have broken the rail and interrupted the electronic circuit on which the signalling system was based. With the circuit broken, the signal at Bayou Sara, a mile and a half up the track, would have shown red rather than the green light that allowed the express through.

Debroah, for one, defends the pilot: 'If you've ever gone up the Mobile river it all looks pretty much the same. There aren't a lot of landmarks. And I think that's why he was confused. The investigation brought out that there were no lights on those bridges because that was not supposed to be a navigable waterway, so you didn't have to light it. That would add to the confusion when the *Mauvilla* lost its way because there was nothing to tell him where he was.'

Moreover, says Randy, 'The fog on the river was so thick that morning that our boats that were responding to the emergency situation had to really slow down. There's always fog on the river in Mobile, Alabama . . .'

9
Spills and Thrills

In the days of sail shipwrecks may have left the shores strewn with spars, bales [and] Bibles . . . but they did not overwhelm miles of coastline with stinking black oil.

E. S. Turner, *London Review of Books*, 22 January 1998

At 9.11 a.m. on the morning of Saturday 18 March 1967 a certain innocence was lost. Until then it had been assumed that the increasingly large oil tankers being built would reduce the cost of petrol and were thus, unequivocally, a Good Thing. Industrially the logic behind such sea-going monsters was impeccable: the bigger the ship, the cheaper it was to transport the oil. Before 1956 the major limitation on the size of tankers *en route* to Europe or the United States from the oilfields of the Middle East had been their ability to pass through the Suez Canal. When this was closed because of the Suez crisis, its importance diminished sharply and the construction of tankers of over 100,000 tons and around 1,000 feet long proceeded apace.

Inevitably, however, these vessels were inherently less strong than their predecessors. Naval architects used stronger steel in an effort to strengthen the ever-longer gaps between 'stiffeners', the heavy brackets which reinforce the ship's structure, but this in turn created problems, notably the instability of the steel panels, and fatigue-cracking where the stresses were greatest. Also, gas built up while the tanks were being cleaned. Eventually this was resolved through the use of inert gases, like nitrogen, in which fire could not survive, but only after a number of massive explosions. The real problem with the supertankers, though, was environmental. Indeed, it is not too much to say that a handful of disasters did more than any other factor to alert the public in industrialized countries to the dangers created by the normal practices of modern industry.

In the past thirty years there have been at least thirty-six oil spills of or above 30,000 tons, but only a handful have impinged on the consciousness of the world's press. It is safe to say that most people will not have heard of the three biggest: the near 300,000 tons spilled by the *Atlantic Express* off Tobago in 1974, the 272,000 tons lost by the *Castillo de Bellver* off Cape Town in 1979, and the 268,000 disgorged tons by the *ABT Summer* in 1991 off the coast of Angola. None affected the wild life or the beaches of the Western world.

Although there had been at least one major spill before 1967 – the *Sinclair Petrolore* had lost 56,000 tons in the Atlantic off Brazil in 1960, though far enough off the coast to avoid any major pollution problems – as far as the Western world was concerned, the decisive moment came when the *Torrey Canyon*, carrying 117,000 tons of heavy Kuwaiti crude oil, struck the rocks off the Scilly Isles. It was undoubtedly one of the crucial moments in the history of environmentalism.

Captain Rugiati was in a hurry. His ship was so heavily loaded that if she did not get to her destination, the deep-water port of Milford Haven in west Wales, by 11 p.m. that Saturday night, she would lose five expensive days because the tides varied so widely – the difference between neap and spring tide was 17 feet.

Unfortunately, in his hurry, he decided to take a short-cut in the channel between Land's End and the Scilly Isles, to the east rather than the west of the Seven Stones light vessel. In theory, the route was clear enough but as the official publication, the *Channel Pilot*, put it:* 'There is no part of the coast of England more subject to sudden changes of weather', so 'The greatest vigilance is necessary and a vessel's position, even in the clearest weather, should be cross-checked at short intervals.'

As the official report on the accident put it:

> The master was imprudent in his decision to pass to the east of the
> Scilly Isles instead of to the west as originally intended. Considering
> the facts that the master's experience in the waters to the east of the
> Islands was very limited and that the *Torrey Canyon* was an
> extremely large and deeply loaded tanker, the Board feels that the
> decision to pass to the east of the Islands exposed the vessel to an
> unnecessary risk which could easily have been avoided.

*Quoted in *Oil & Water – The Torrey Canyon Disaster*, Edward Cowan, William Kimber, London, 1969.

Within a few minutes, in Cowan's words, 'With a grinding screech the *Torrey Canyon* tore her bottom open on Pollard Rock, granite harder than steel. Crude oil poured into the sea just sixteen miles from the most popular holiday resort in England.'

The innocence of the times is best shown by the slowness of the official response to the disaster which would have been unthinkable a decade later. In a pub at lunch-time the local MP, John Nott, was told of the disaster, but no one seemed to think it important, and although the *Observer* the next day headlined its report 'Oil Threatens Holiday Beaches' the story was tucked away at the bottom of the front page. Indeed, the eventual full-hearted response would not have been as great if the Prime Minister, Harold Wilson, had not had a holiday cottage on the Scilly Isles.

As it was, it was not until Sunday lunch-time, after attempts to refloat the tanker had failed, that Harold Wilson contacted Maurice Foley, the parliamentary under-secretary for the Royal Navy, and sent him to Cornwall. By then a leading salvage expert had been killed in an explosion that remains a mystery to this day. The only effective remedial measures being applied were that three naval vessels had been spraying detergent on the spreading patch of oil but the navy doubted it could be used in large enough quantities to avert large-scale oil pollution. By Sunday afternoon the slick measured 18 by 4 miles and, close to the tanker, was as much as 18 inches thick. It was an unprecedented situation and no one had a clue as to the best course of action. 'Oil pollution like this had never occurred, anywhere,' wrote Cowan. 'The navy inclined to the view that extraordinary action was needed to cope with an extraordinary situation. It recommended that the tanker and her cargo be burned.' *The Times* likened the spraying exercise to 'trying to mop the Kensington Round Pond dry with a sponge'.

It was already clear that trying to empty the oil from the tanker would take an immensely long time: the ship's own pumps were out of action, and finding enough hoses to cope with pumping out the remaining 800,000 tons of oil on the ship and fixing them to a stranded ship in a rough sea was not a practical solution in the time available – it would have taken a month to pump out all the oil and no one believed that the tanker would remain afloat that long.

More drastic action would involve blowing up the tanker, which would, in theory, result in horrendous legal complications. As Cowan put it:

When the *Torrey Canyon* hit Pollard Rock there was no relevant experience, statute, convention or court case to which the government could turn for guidance. Add to these ingredients the British respect for property rights and due process of law, and it is understandable that the Wilson government let the choice of remedy rest with the ship's owner and did not take a more radical course in an unexpected, strange crisis.

By the middle of the following week, Wilson had finally enlisted the country's best scientific brains to try to cope with the crisis in a committee headed by Sir Solly Zuckerman, the government's chief scientific advisor. By then it was clear that the tanker could not be refloated and that the only effective solution was to destroy it. 'In eight and a half days of hammering,' wrote Cowan, 'the wind and the sea had claimed their biggest prize in man's many centuries of seafaring.'

The only practical solution seemed to be to set the oil alight by bombing the by now wrecked tanker. Tests seemed to prove that the thick crude oil could be ignited and the navy and Royal Air Force attempted to do this while it was still contained in the tanks on the ship. This, it was reasoned, would release the lighter and more combustible components in a sort of refining process. With the use of high-explosive bombs, aviation fuel and napalm, they managed to get rid of most of the oil on the ship.

This left the considerable problem of the oil that had leaked from the ship. This was the first battle against pollution and everyone was in the dark as to how to proceed. They did not know the long-term effects either of the oil or of the chemical detergents used to clean it up.

It was soon established that some of the most heavily vaunted methods for coping with the problem were of limited, if any, use. Booms to stop the spread of the oil, and devices to suck it up would obviously work only in calm conditions, unlikely to be found round any oil spill. The best method for absorbing the oil was in 'scavenging devices', hay, straw, or, even better, leather shavings, which absorbed the oil but not the water, to as much as ten times their dry weight. Afterwards they could be taken ashore and burned. Before the *Torrey Canyon* ran aground these absorbents had been widely used by oil companies and harbour authorities but only when they were faced with much smaller spillages. The only hope, however, with so big a spill as that from the *Torrey Canyon* was to use chemical detergent in massive amounts – nearly 3,500 tons were used in the *Torrey Canyon* rescue bid and that was reckoned to have emulsified only 15,000 tons of oil, leaving another 20,000 tons to be washed ashore. Once that happened only human muscle power, spades, buckets and brooms offered any real hope. Even then another problem emerged: the formation of the so-called 'chocolate mousse'. Technically this consisted of emulsions of water in oil and water droplets surrounded by oil which formed a thick chocolate-coloured jelly. This did not burn easily and required further – expensive – treatment with detergents.

Three separate battles took place. The first, the most-publicized and thus the one to which most effort was devoted, was on the beaches. The use of detergents sometimes proved counter-productive: it helped to saturate the sand with the oil, which had sometimes penetrated the sand before the rescuers had started work. 'Sometimes,' wrote Cowan, 'the sea washed out several feet of sand and exposed pools of oil and water the colour of melted baking chocolate and rocks covered with darker, semi-solid oil.'

Nevertheless the heroic and expensive efforts made by the military and civilian authorities ensured that, by the following summer, Cornwall's precious beaches, the foundation of its economy, had recovered. But the government's scientific advisers were also fully aware of the other two battles they faced resulting from the damage caused to marine and bird life by the detergent. Their own report stated plainly that 'It was fully appreciated that there would be substantial losses among inter-tidal animals, and probably some deaths locally of crabs and lobsters, but it was felt that these losses could be accepted in the circumstances.' By implication, the losses were bearable compared with 'the advantages to the holiday industry in cleaning the beaches'. In any case, the damage would be minimized by 'the immense volume of sea off Cornwall, the great tidal mixing that occurs twice a day and the frequency of rough seas at this time of year'. For once the authorities were proved right – though only after an anxious few months for Cornwall's fishermen. But, as Sir Solly Zuckerman's committee pointed out: 'There are few areas round Britain with correspondingly favourable topographic and other environmental characteristics where oil and detergent would have done so little damage to fisheries.' This statement was the beginning of a learning curve that assumed much greater importance in later years: that the authorities should not try to impose artificial solutions on artificial problems, but should leave the solution as far as possible to nature, with its own capacity for absorbing new pollutants and rendering them harmless.

Indeed, the researchers soon became aware of the side-effects of the detergents. They thinned the oil, so that it spread further and made it easier for sea-life to ingest the deadly compounds of oil and detergent, whereas, as a local naturalist pointed out, 'Even where there was gross oil pollution the shore life was surprisingly healthy.' His judgement was backed by the Zuckerman committee, which confirmed that the mix of oil and detergent did 'widespread damage to inter-tidal marine plant and animal life'. To which a local councillor, Stuart Kneebone, replied forcefully that 'Something or someone has to pay a price in "blood" in any battle. I would rather see inshore marine life and wild birds pay with their blood than human beings, perhaps not directly but indirectly, maybe in happiness and a continuing enjoyment of a clean coastline.'

The biggest – and most British – wave of concern was not so much for the crabs and limpets but for the thousands of birds killed or crippled by the oil. Although massive efforts were devoted to cleaning them it was reckoned that only one in a hundred that had been treated – and they represented less than a quarter of the total affected – could be returned to the sea with any hope of survival. Even here, though, the effect was relatively short-term with other birds returning the next year.

It soon became clear that, with the growth in the number of super-tankers, the *Torrey Canyon* was merely the first of many disasters waiting to happen the world over. In early March the following year, 1968, the Liberian tanker *Ocean Eagle* broke in two off Puerto Rico. The harbour was covered with a one-inch layer of oil that spread for ten miles along the north coast of the island, ruining the tourist beaches. During the subsequent investigations, the first mate admitted that the tanker had been overloaded, with the cargo seven inches above its legal limit. Less than a week later the Greek tanker *General Colocotronis* had struck a reef off the Bahamas, causing a five-mile-long slick on the beaches of Eleuthera island.

Eleven years after the *Torrey Canyon* disaster had first woken the world to the potential dangers from oil pollution came one of the worst disasters of them all: the wreck of the supertanker *Amoco Cadiz* on the shores of Brittany, spilling 223,000 tons of crude oil on to the beaches of north-western France. The disaster showed clearly that the slightest hesitation in calling for help once a tanker goes out of control can have a fatal impact on the environment.

The ship's steering engine broke down at 0946 on the morning of 16 March 1978 eight miles off the island of Ushant after two days of rough weather and heavy seas. Because of the presence of other westbound ships, she was already a mile closer to shore than she should have been when she became uncontrollable.

The cause of the breakdown was that the port-side flange of the four pipes leading from the pumps to the distribution block was not secure and oil was being pumped out at high pressure. In difficult and dangerous conditions the crew tried to repair the flanges and the broken studs that should have secured the flange to the distribution block, but they did not succeed.

Unfortunately the master, Captain Badari, failed to take decisive action. Immediately after the accident he ordered a 'Not Under Command' signal to be hoisted and stated that he sent out a radio message saying that he had steering problems and warning other ships to keep clear. But he admitted that he did not at this stage think of requesting assistance. By the time he did, at 1100, it was too late. The salvage tug *Pacific*, which came to the rescue, had passed close to the *Amoco Cadiz* earlier that day and the court of inquiry believed that had her captain asked for help, she, with the much larger *Simson* – which in the event arrived too late to be of any use – could have rescued the stricken tanker.

Even when contact had been made between the tug and the tanker, the captains had a long discussion about salvage terms – the captain of the *Amoco Cadiz* only wanted a tow, the captain of the tug wanted an open salvage agreement. To make matters worse they were negotiating in English, a language foreign to both men, and Captain Badari felt he had to refer the whole matter to his head office in Chicago, causing an even longer delay. Nevertheless, the *Pacific* succeeded in establishing a towline to get the tanker on to a more westerly course away from the shore. But the weather was atrocious and after three hours the towline snapped, leaving the tanker drifting inexorably towards the coast at the mercy of the wind and the tide. Later that evening, its engines were stopped and the *Pacific* tried to attach another towline but did not have the pulling power required by the size of the tanker and the appalling weather conditions. By 2100 that evening the tanker had struck a reef unmarked on any charts and immediately started to leak. The next morning it broke in two and, as Norman Hooke* puts it, 'A

*op. cit.

blackish-brown tide of crude oil spilled forth from the ripped tanks to cover the Brittany coast with approximately 223,000 tons of disastrous filthy ooze'. In all, the oil slick covered about 125 miles of that coast.

The French authorities were totally unprepared for such a monumental disaster. In 1970 their basic plan had been drawn up to deal with a maximum spill of 30,000 tons, a seventh of the total that oozed from the *Amoco Cadiz*, and although the plan had been updated three months earlier the local authorities were not aware of the changes. Twelve days after the accident the tanker broke into three while the French Navy dropped depth charges to release the rest of the oil under controlled conditions.

The delays in organizing help resulted in riots by locals whose living was threatened by the pollution, leading to desperate efforts to attack the oil with detergent. The French mobilized thousands of troops and civilian volunteers to remove much of the oil, literally by hand, from Brittany's finest tourist beaches in an emergency effort known as 'Operation Teaspoon'. The slick not only affected the tourist trade: like the *Torrey Canyon* disaster, it ruined the livelihood of hundreds of local fishermen by killing the shellfish and the white fish like whiting on which they depended for a living – and, inevitably, the French public became wary of Brittany's beaches and seafood long after the clean-up had been completed.

The spill resulted in another, surprising, economic disaster: the seaweed, too, was polluted. It was a valuable commodity, because the locals had collected and sold it for use in cosmetics and speciality chemicals. A fortnight later in an ironical postscript, a Danish ship, the *Henriette Bravo*, which was being used to carry seaweed affected by the accident out to deep water for dumping, sank because the seaweed shifted in her hold. But, as in so many other such cases, nature proved resilient and, within three years, most of the major pollution effects had disappeared.

The Americans' worst environmental disaster – which, however, rank only thirty-fifth in the league table of 'Big Spills' – came about with the spillage of 36,000 tons of oil from the tanker *Exxon Valdez* when it ran aground on Bligh Reef in Alaska's Prince William Sound nine minutes after midnight on 24 March 1989. It was by no means the first such incident to threaten the shores of the USA. In December 1976 the 28,000-ton tanker *Argo Merchant* had run aground near Nantucket, split into three sections and spilt virtually all its cargo. Ecological disaster threatened but was averted by wind, which blew the oil safely offshore.

Many worse spills outside American waters never reached the newspapers. For example, 50,000 tons of crude oil had been spilt in the Magellan Straits in 1968 when the tanker *Metula* ran aground. Although the desolate region is almost uninhabited, it houses an enormous wealth of sea-life, yet the accident passed almost unnoticed – except by the fish.

In the affair of the *Exxon Valdez*, the American legal system, the greed of many plaintiffs and the company Exxon's initial refusal to take the situation seriously enough succeeded in blowing the case out of all proportion. One judge even compared the spill – in which no one was injured, let alone killed – to the bombing of Hiroshima, and said that it was worse even than the way in which Saddam Hussein had set fire to a hundred and fifty times as much oil as was spilt in Prince William Sound.

But the wrecking of the *Valdez* was a surprise. When Steve McCall, the senior coastguard officer in Valdez, Alaska, was woken up to be told of the disaster 'my initial reaction was shock', he recalls. In hindsight, says McCall, 'it's one of those things where if someone had come to make a disaster movie and said we have this scenario of good visibility, nothing mechanically wrong, an American flagship, very qualified people going around some ice, what do you think? I would have said no, the real scenario would be miserable night, rainy, snowy, poor visibility, something going wrong mechanically and running aground while you're aiming to go through the Narrows.'

The handling of the *Exxon Valdez* affair showed everyone involved in a bad light: the harbour and pipeline authorities were incompetent and unprepared for any such incident; the American legal system was slow, expensive and largely pointless; Exxon was legalistic and at first unable to comprehend the extent of the disaster, and the reporting by the American media was pious and inaccurate. Even the locals were revealed as greedy and quarrelsome.

The tanker was on a routine trip from Alaska to California. After the local pilot had left and as she set off down Prince William Sound and along Valdez Arm to the open sea, the master, Captain Hazelwood, gave precise instructions on the change of course to Greg Cousins, the third mate, before retiring below. A quarter of an hour later the tanker hit a series of reef pinnacles before grinding to a halt on a narrow ledge with a 600-foot gash in her bottom.

Lieutenant Commander Tom Falkenstein, who at the time was the executive officer at the Coastguard Marine Safety Office in Valdez, 'concluded that the ship had gone over a rock then landed on a shallower rock and that's where she perched on the number two and number three cargo tanks. We had no idea of the extent of the damage, other than that the ship had been severely holed, because the chief mate said that the levels in the cargo tanks were dropping faster than he had ever seen them load and they load about 150,000 to 200,000 barrels an hour.'

The grounding couldn't have happened at a worse place or at a worse time. As Steve McCall explains: 'Bligh Reef itself, the portion where the *Exxon Valdez* ran aground, is not visible, the rocks are fifty feet below the surface of the water, so in your average boat you could go over those rocks and never even know they were there. Of course, the *Valdez* was drawing more water than that. Unfortunately when she ran aground it was just about at full tide. And she didn't get stuck on one rock pinnacle but two. And before she got stuck, she travelled over those rocks, puncturing eleven cargo tanks. With the bottom ripped open, as the tide dropped, the oil ran out. So in the six- or seven-hour period during that first tide cycle, over 200,000 barrels of oil came out of the ship. And during those first six or seven hours, that first tide cycle, people were concerned about the ship breaking up.'

The undisputed series of events soon gave rise to a dozen questions. The first, and most elementary, concerned whether there should have been a pilot on board. Tom Falkenstein distinguishes between state and federal regulations, which were applicable if, as in the case of the *Exxon Valdez*, the ship was travelling between American ports. As a result, he says, 'Greg Cousins couldn't have been piloting the ship legally without Captain Hazelwood, who was the only one on the bridge who held a pilot's endorsement for Prince William Sound'. Ironically, the qualification, which Cousins did not have, would not have been necessary had new rules, already drawn up, been applied.

Next, the ship had sailed into an area normally off-limits to tankers while trying to avoid large lumps of floating ice in Prince William Sound. She had asked the coastguard for permission to move from the outgoing to the incoming lane to avoid the ice, then strayed across the incoming lane. Falkenstein emphasizes that 'It was not unusual for a ship to wander out of the lanes to avoid chunks of ice. That had been going on all year. Six weeks earlier another Exxon ship had advised us that there was a lot of ice coming out of those lanes. These chunks of ice, by the way, coming out of Columbia glacier, are not *Titanic* ship-killers; they're maybe fifteen or twenty feet across, and thirty or forty feet long. They are not monsters, they cause dents. If they're hit they could cause a small hole.' To McCall, the change of course seemed natural: 'There was no other traffic in the lane, coming in or going out, so he had the whole road, so to speak, to himself. Like, if you're driving down a road and you see some rocks ahead of you, do you slow down and try to drive over them, maybe punch a hole in your tyre, or scratch your paint, or gee whiz, realize no one's going the other way, swing out around the rocks and go into the opposite lane of traffic, fully intending to come back into your lane? That kind of parallel scenario.'

But the biggest question mark hung over the captain. When the tanker grounded, wrote Daniel Coyle,* the captain, Joseph Hazelwood 'was transfigured from an anonymous but skilled professional into a lasting national symbol of rank incompetence and drunk idiocy'. The classic, mistaken version of the accident came in a page-one analysis in the *New York Times*: that Hazelwood had 'probably' set the ship on autopilot and gone below – probably to sleep off a hangover incurred by a drunken binge ashore – while the third mate, Greg Cousins, and the helmsman, Robert Kagan, 'desperately tried' to regain control. The legend then recounts how, unaware that several large steel plates had come loose – one measuring 70 feet square – while three rocks, one described as 'half the size of a house', had become embedded in her hull, Hazelwood had then tried to power the ship off the reef, spilling yet more millions of gallons of oil.

There was a belief that Hazelwood, strictly against regulations, had had a drink or two. 'The alcohol became an issue,' says Falkenstein. 'When I walked up and spoke with Captain Hazelwood and noticed the odour of alcohol in the immediate vicinity of only the captain, it was a logical conclusion that he had been drinking. I dismissed it in the back of my mind as being the action of a man who had just seen his career go down the tubes and so he had gone and had a drink. Mark Delozier, another Valdez coastguard, looked at it from a different viewpoint.' He decided that: 'What we needed to do was conduct these tests. We didn't have the test equipment with us. The Supreme Court had only ruled maybe ten days earlier that the federal laws governing alcohol testing of individuals involved in accidents

*In *Outside* magazine, October 1997.

were constitutional.' To get the test equipment on board meant contacting their commanding officer then sending for a state trooper, who thought they wanted to arrest someone and at first didn't bring his breathalyser kit. They hauled a visiting hospital technician off a plane and finally performed the tests eleven hours later. The blood alcohol and urine tests required in such situations were not taken until ten hours after the grounding. Despite the lack of any evidence from a breathalyser or an immediate blood test Dr Malcolm Brenner, one of the investigators, believed that the captain was drunk or, in his words, 'had probably consumed an amount of ethanol sufficient to affect his speech in several ways: considerable word interjections, broken words, incomplete phrases, corrected errors and hesitations'. He backed up his conclusions with frequency measurement of the tape, making comparisons of various words and phrases as Hazelwood had uttered them the day before the accident, an hour before, at the time of the accident, and an hour later.

The case for the defence begins with a crucial five-minute gap after Hazelwood told Cousins to change course and nothing was done. 'The reason Greg Cousins didn't make the turn is not real clear in the National Transportation Safety Board report,' says Falkenstein. 'I believe it was because he wasn't absolutely sure where the ship was. He was attempting to fix the ship's position by taking bearings to certain known objects. He would take a bearing to two lights and a radar range to a particular point of land. And the ship is moving while the bearing is being taken. So you want to take those readings quickly, record them, then make your drawings on the chart. I think it took Greg Cousins somewhere between seven and ten minutes to take those bearings,' during which time the ship had travelled well over a nautical mile. 'He didn't really have a good idea where that ship actually was in that Sound and then as a result he didn't know exactly when to make his turn, and I think that is the single most important contributing factor to why she didn't turn in time.'

An NTSB investigator, Richard Johnson, pointed out that there were not enough people on the bridge at the critical time and that Cousins had been working long hours without sleep. At the critical moments he took two phone calls and was trying to plot a course with his back to the bow of the ship while the watch-officer, Maureen Jones, was telling him about the dangerous proximity of the warning buoy on Bligh Reef.

Hazelwood's case, which was eventually accepted even by the coastguard, is put by Coyle. 'He was neither drunk nor negligent. The real reason for the accident lies in an unfortunate combination of mundane events, happenstance, and human mistakes – the most significant of which were not made by Hazelwood.' In the courts it was Cousins who accepted much of the blame for failing to execute the change of course Hazelwood had ordered, and failing to check that the helmsman – whose records showed that he 'required constant supervision' - had followed the orders. Hazelwood says simply that he left the bridge 'because there wasn't a compelling reason to stay'. Nevertheless, as even his friends agreed, he wasn't there when he should have been. As Captain Russ Nyborg, a friend quoted by Coyle, put it, 'He left it to somebody else and somebody else screwed up. Joe should have watched his mate a little closer.' Nor had Hazelwood tried to 'power' the ship off the reef, merely called for forward throttle to keep it hard up against the reef to stop the bleeding.

The blood test, which allegedly showed his alcohol level, involved so many irregularities that at best it was a bad joke, and dozens of witnesses attested that his behaviour had not been impaired by alcohol. (The assumption of drunkenness was based on the fact that he had been on a rehabilitation programme some years earlier.) The media ignored the fact that the spill-control equipment was in an appalling state, and that Exxon, the state and the pipeline authorities converted a crisis into a catastrophe by their ditherings. Hazelwood's appearance – his shadowy beard, his stubborn lip – did not help his case and he appeared to confirm his guilt in steadfastly refusing to talk about the incident. 'His silence,' wrote Coyle, 'rescued Exxon, which needed a bogeyman; the press, which needed a reason; and the public, which needed a way to think about the unthinkable.' He had not helped his case by his reply – 'You're looking at it' – to two coastguard officers who asked him what the problem was. 'It wasn't an admission of guilt,' he told Coyle, 'but everyone interpreted it as such.' At his first trial Hazelwood went on the offensive, claiming immunity because he had, supposedly, reported the spill. This was dismissed by a judge, who said that other people would have reported the spill too. The next year Hazelwood was found guilty on the most minor of the charges alleged against him, negligent discharge of oil, and was given a suspended prison sentence. Yet he continued the battle to clear his name, and in 1992 the Alaskan appellate court overturned his conviction, ruling that the prosecutors had used 'tainted evidence'. Meanwhile, the verdict of the NTSB concluded that the probable cause of the grounding of the *Exxon Valdez* was the failure of the third mate to manoeuvre the vessel properly because of fatigue and excessive workload; the failure of the master, Hazelwood, to provide a proper navigation watch because his judgement was impaired through alcohol; the failure of Exxon to provide a fit master and an adequate crew.

On the afternoon of the spill another Exxon tanker managed to manoeuvre alongside the *Exxon Valdez* and remove much of the 900,000 barrels of oil that remained in its holds, which emphasized that if the captain had acted earlier the disaster would have been greatly diminished. Unfortunately the spill had occurred in an enclosed stretch of water, thus preventing the sea from helping in the clear-up process in a sound that was accessible only by air or sea. To make matters worse, the waters were a reservoir of fish stocks, ranging from whales to shrimp, crab and oysters – and some of the world's largest salmon hatcheries.

In theory, the booms and skimmers held in reserve for such an emergency should have been in place within five hours of an accident but the barge used to carry the equipment was being repaired at the time, thus delaying its deployment. When the local emergency teams did begin work they found that the water was too calm for the chemical dispersants employed, which required rough conditions to mix with the oil.

Two quite separate battles soon developed. The first was over the clean-up. The remaining oil had been pumped from the tanker's hold within a few weeks but this had left an oil slick covering over one thousand miles of shoreline. Over a hundred vessels were initially deployed in the operation, costing Exxon over a million dollars a day. By the end of the summer – at which point Exxon temporarily abandoned a clean-up that had involved 48,000 workers and a total of 1,300 boats – nearly 1,100 miles of Prince William Sound and the Gulf of Alaska were reported tainted. Exxon claimed that its workers had recovered about 60,000 barrels of oil, though the local department of conservation estimated the total at only 32,500 barrels, leaving 147,000 barrels on the beaches. Eighteen months later, it was said that 85 per cent of the affected beaches had been cleaned. But the disaster had cost the lives of as many as 580,000 birds and over 5,500 sea otters. The last crews were only demobilized three years after the disaster in July 1991 when the total cost had reached over $2.5 billion.

Much longer drawn-out, more complex and more expensive were the legal battles, which lasted seven years. These became inconceivably tangled.

Within a month of the accident thirty-one lawsuits and 1,300 claims, ranging from $500 to $4 million, and totallying $10 billion, had been filed against Exxon. The claims alleged damage and ill-health caused to the inhabitants as a whole, including separate suits filed on behalf of a group of 10,000 fishermen, twelve Alaskan communities, and a group of 4,000 individual Alaskan natives.

Exxon had the worst of all possible worlds. When it finally grasped the enormity of the problems that it faced, the machinery of American legal process was in action, and all offers the company made, however apparently generous, were treated as inadequate. It did not help that Exxon's legal attitude throughout can be described only as belligerent. It sued the state of Alaska for not allowing it to use dispersants for two crucial days and the US Coastguard for $2 billion as being partially responsible.

In September 1990, a judge ruled that Exxon was liable for all the damage caused. By then the company had spent over $2 billion on the clean-up and had paid over $240 million in claims. Six months later, a settlement between Exxon, the federal government and the state of Alaska came unstuck when the state legislature asked for the several billion dollars owing to be paid more quickly, with $1.2 billion to be handed over in the first year. The two plaintiffs reached an agreement in the August of 1991 and by October Exxon had pleaded guilty to four environmental crimes and had paid over $1 billion to the state.

But this left two other problems: the civil suits and the insurers. In 1993, the insurers weighed in with a belated attempt to ensure that they were not held liable for the disaster. In 1994 a federal jury in Anchorage ruled that Exxon and the master were guilty of negligence and that damages of up to $15 billion would be awarded. But within a few months it became clear that the numerous interests involved – from crab and shrimp fishermen to salmon and herring fishermen – would receive only a fraction of the enormous sums they had claimed. Only in October 1996 did Exxon strike a deal with the insurers who paid $480 million towards the company's costs on top of an earlier payment of $300 million, a fraction of their original claim.

As always, a number of locks were fitted on the tanker door after the oil had bolted. In 1990 a new Oil Pollution Act was passed. Falkenstein reveals that: 'Prior to the *Exxon Valdez* going aground, the operations officer and the senior chief petty officer in radar operations both decided that they would make it a matter of routine for the operators to monitor ships as they went down Valdez Arm until they lost contact with them on the radar. That, the unit did on its own without guidance. That's what was being done that night. The radar operator lost contact, logged the range and position when he lost contact, and forgot about the ship. That was the procedure at the time. In 1987 the unit suffered cuts in the number of staff provided in the vessel-traffic service. In 1989, after this incident occurred, those staff were restored and better radar installed.'

Another result was the provision of escort tugs for all tankers in Prince William Sound, a measure that Falkenstein, for one, dismisses as useless. 'The ships are so large and travel at such a speed that an escort tug is rather limited in what it can do to help a tanker that loses steering.' On the other hand, 'The requirement for pollution equipment to be on site in Valdez, for the stationing of pollution equipment at various locations in various ports, the establishment of coastguard strike teams with pollution equipment to respond to emergencies, those are all good things. When the *Exxon Valdez* went aground, the pollution equipment that the coastguard had was adequate for a small harbour spill. We did not have enough pollution equipment on scene for that size of incident, neither did Alaska Marine Terminal.

'Since the *Exxon Valdez* there has been a lot more pollution equipment on site. Had the same circumstances existed at the time, the spill might have been contained more readily. Would these circumstances have prevented the tanker from going aground? I don't believe so. They'd have been witnesses to the incident. Maybe they'd have forced the mate to be a little more alert. I don't believe they could have done anything more to prevent an accident. Could they have gathered up the oil? They could have gathered up some of it, but the equipment didn't exist and the coastguard didn't have anything on scene. We had what I've referred to as a low-ball poker hand in a high-ball game and we weren't about to win with what we'd been dealt.'

In January 1993 the weather in the Shetlands was unusually bad. Magnus Flaws, an auxiliary coastguard, reckons, 'It was the worst January we'd ever seen. There were something like twenty-eight gales, ten storms and four hurricanes. The wind blew non-stop.' Not that the weather in the Shetlands is kind at the best of times. As Friedie Manson, an experienced helicopter winchman, explains: 'Shetland is an island. You've got the North Sea on the east side and the Atlantic Ocean to the west side, two different seas, the conditions can vary quite a lot. The one thing in Shetland, as anybody around here will tell you, is that the weather can change within a couple of hours and you can really have all four seasons in one day quite easily.'

To make matters worse, as James Dickson, then port-safety manager and oil-pollution control at Sullom Voe, points out, 'Shetland is 60 degrees north so we're the same latitude as Greenland, the same latitude as Alaska. The nearest land is about a hundred miles away, so you have a large fetch – the distance of sea between you and the next bit of land. If you have a very severe wind it will build up into a swell and that swell gets bigger and bigger and bigger, and it's not unusual for us to have swells in excess of fifteen, twenty metres. In a very bad gale, if you use your imagination, you'll see the white crests of the waves as they curl. Green water is where the ship is digging in and lifting thousands of tons of water bodily, just pure water, no foam, no spray, no nothing.'

On 3 January the Liberian-registered tanker *Braer*, loaded with 84,500 tons of North Sea oil, set out from the Norwegian port of Mongstad *en route* for Quebec. A force-10 gale was blowing. The ship was travelling at no more than 2.5 knots and rolling badly in thirty-foot waves.

Around midnight the chief engineer reported that the fuel supply was contaminated with sea-water. Attempts to purify it failed, and at 0440 on 5 January the engine broke down. After drifting helplessly for three-quarters of an hour in forty-foot waves, the captain called his head office. The coastguard picked up his call and contacted him. Even then he could have avoided the accident. As one of the investigators from the MAIB (Marine Accident Investigation Branch), David Dunn, pointed out: 'The master should have used the magnetic compass, which is required to be provided on a ship for situations such as this when main power is lost. If he had used it and taken bearings of shore lights – and the visibility was quite good for the time – he could have ascertained his position, concluded from that the rate of drift, and given coastguards perhaps better information as to what was likely to happen.'

At first, Captain Gelis said he needed a tugboat because the engine had broken down, but he was unclear on whether he was prepared to pay the full commercial rate for the tow: 'I don't know if you can make arrangements for the tug,' he told the coastguard, 'because just now I haven't contacted my owners.' His response was typical of a captain of a ship belonging to one of the smaller shipping companies. They are invariably unwilling to incur the considerable expense of hiring an ocean-going tug.

Gordon Downard, the coastguard officer on duty, says: 'There were language problems, and we weren't talking to the same person all the time. One time it might be the captain, or the second officer, or the third mate. We went back on numerous occasions asking if they'd contact their owners for permission to mobilize the tugs. Even though we had made the phone calls here to the tug companies, advising them of the situation and getting them going, we'd had to get that clarification that they were agreeing to the towing.'

At 0625 the coastguard made a Pan Pan call, indicating problems but not the full-scale emergency of the Mayday signal. By first light the *Braer* had drifted ten miles back towards the Shetlands. At 0812 the captain said he didn't want to abandon ship, even though he had been warned by the pilot of a rescue helicopter that the ship would run aground an hour later. Jonathan Wills, a freelance journalist based in the Shetlands, throws more light on the captain's reluctance to call a tug: 'There's also professional embarrassment and bad publicity, because what goes through the local coastguard station gets in the local radio and newspapers and, thanks to people like me, it'll get in the national newspapers as well.'

A spectacular effort ensured that none of the crew died in the subsequent disaster. Friedie Manson says: 'It was black dark by the time we went out. When we got on scene, there were very high seas and there was swell about the size of a house. The wind speed was about force-10 gale, which is approximately 60 miles an hour. The ship herself had no engine power and her only lighting was emergency lights dotted around the main structure. We used our own lights from the helicopter to illuminate the winching area. A couple of times I was waist deep in water, which is quite a lot of water, and I could just get across the deck. At that time you really had to hold on to the rails and just hang on for grim life. We got the crew to muster down on the stern of the vessel, sheltering behind the structure, and once I got them briefed we managed to get them winched up into the aircraft.'

For James Dickson it was the first day at work after the New Year break. At 5.30 a.m., he recalls, 'I was woken by a call from Captain Sullivan, the director of marine operations, saying that there was a vessel in distress to the south of Shetland and in danger of coming ashore. We had her position and we knew the wind speed and direction so it was very easy to plot that on the chart and have a look how she was going to drift. It became painfully obvious that she was going to end up on Shetland. We have a Volko 105 helicopter, which is on permanent charter to us for pollution surveillance and surveillance of shipping and pilotage, so we called the helicopter crew in. They came in about seven and the aircraft was prepared to take off at first light, which is about eight o'clock. I went with the helicopter and flew down to Sumburgh. We got there about eight-thirty, there was a lot of wind so we made slow progress heading towards the south. When we got within a couple of miles of the *Braer* we could see her rolling heavily. By that time the crew had all been winched off and she was just totally dead there, unmanned. It was fairly obvious that she was going to go ashore near Sumburgh Head. We went down to refuel at Sumburgh.'

There was a short delay while they got hold of a couple of crew members. 'We wanted them to come with us,' says Dickson, 'because they were familiar with the layout of the ship.' The delay was criticized later. As David Dunn put it, 'The coastguard perhaps didn't appreciate the urgency of the situation at that time, but having said that it's fair to say that the master had not transmitted a formal urgency message. Nevertheless, the master had asked for towage assistance, and the coastguard didn't perhaps place quite the priority that was needed in that particular case.' As soon as they were assembled they took off in the search-and-rescue helicopter, Oscar Charlie.

Dickson still believed that 'If we got on board now we might be able to try and do something.' They decided 'that the best plan would be to actually winch down to the after-end and to see if we could attach a towline and very gently try and bring the stern into the wind to stop the drift again. It was just to hold position until the cavalry came over the hillside because there were all kinds of tugs and vessels trying to come down to give assistance. I went down with Friedie Manson and two crew members from the *Braer*, which by this time was about 50 metres off the shore. She was moving terribly fast towards the beach. I thought maybe the backwash was keeping her off because you can imagine the waves were crashing into the rocks and there was a reflected wave going in the other direction. I thought perhaps she might stay there long enough to try and get these wires attached, so we winched down.'

Dickson dismisses the idea that he was descending into a dangerous situation. 'At the time it's all exciting and there's a lot of adrenaline flowing and you just get on with it and see what happens. I think the most important thing was Oscar Charlie being there. That crew is probably the most experienced search-and-rescue helicopter team in the world so it's always handy to know that they're up there to come and get you off, if and when it all goes wrong! At the time we went on board the *Braer* seemed to be more or less steady, but she must have been inching her way towards the shore. But, I must admit, my attention was always to seaward and not landward.'

By that time a powerful tug, the *Star Sirius*, had arrived on the scene. If she had been called earlier she might have been able to save the *Braer*. According to Dickinson, she 'came in stern first towards the *Braer*, about 50 metres off'. At the second attempt the tug managed to land a line on the *Braer*, but it 'went over the bridge and unfortunately got tangled up in the lifeboat and the bridge itself so I had to go along the port-side where there were no rails at all and the sea was still being washed up so I had to pick my moment when I ran along the deck. We got the line, managed to cut it free from the bits of rigging and eventually got it back down on the deck again and to the stern of the ship, where we then started to try to pull it across. It was very difficult to pull the heavy rope through the water. We managed to get about 30 metres' worth across. By this time the vessel was getting very close to the rocks and the tug decided it was unsafe for them to stay with her. It was elected that they had to pull away and we had to give up.'

As the two crew members were being winched off, a huge wave 'lifted the whole vessel up and just set it right down on the rocks with a great thud. The whole thing juddered to a halt and everything shook about us. You could feel the shudder, a very pronounced shudder, and you could see all the bits of masts and aerials, antennae and wires sort of vibrating. I could see the black oil coming out already. She was losing her bunkers because I think she touched aft first and punctured the bunker tanks and you could see that it was all lost.' It happened very quickly. They were on board for a mere fifteen minutes and when she hit the rocks, their only thought was to get off 'because there's nothing you can do then. It was clear she'd been holed – you could smell the oil for a start – and once she loses buoyancy that's it, game, set and match. Just forget it, try and get off.'

An oil spill twice the size of that produced by the *Exxon Valdez* had begun to spread. Friedie Manson describes how 'She broke up over the space of a week, the *Braer*. The first day or two she stayed fairly well contained within herself, except she had been holed underneath in the hull. Then she broke up over the next two or three days, and by the end of the week she was smashed to pieces, because we had a week of violent storm-force gales. She took a real hammering and broke up quite bad.'

Fortunately the *Braer* had sunk in the least dangerous conditions in which spills should occur: the power of the sea, which had originally caused the trouble, could be relied on to cope with the result of the devastation for which it had been responsible. In the days following the disaster, says Magnus Flaws, the water in the bays round the wreck was brown. 'The waves were actually breaking brown, going up on to the sand. The crude oil mixed in with the sea and it just washed back off the beach again. It didn't leave any deposits on the beach. The only deposit being left was the fuel oil, but a lot of people were cleaning it up so it didn't last too long. Nature took over and the strength of the sea and the wind dispersed it. So we were very lucky with the type of oil that was on the vessel. [It was light crude from the Norwegian sector of the North Sea.] It could have been really heavy crude oil and I imagine we'd maybe still have been cleaning this place up, but now it's pristine, the waters are clean, there's no pollution whatsoever.' Nevertheless, the initial impact on the shore – and the birds – had been severe and the international compensation fund ended up paying £35 million to fishermen for the destruction of the season's haul of salmon.

During the investigations that followed the disaster, Alan Rushton of the MAIB noticed a curious point about the fuel measurements in the tank. 'The fuel goes from the engine-oil tank to a settling tank then through a purifier to a service tank. Now, the *Braer* used a ton of fuel an hour with a gauge reading of 9.5 tons in the service tank. After three hours it was still reading eight tons, way above what it should normally have been. The tank was contaminated with sea-water, which they knew. But no one had asked where the sea-water was coming from.' Meanwhile David Dunn interviewed the captain and the chief officer, and discovered that pipes stored on deck had broken free and were rolling around loose. The chief officer had noticed them the previous morning but it was too dangerous to send anyone on deck to secure them. The pipes had broken the oil-tank air-vents, allowing sea-water to flood into the fuel tanks.

The MAIB report severely criticized the master. 'When it was reported to the master that the pipe sections had broken loose, he failed to take any action to try to have them rescued or simply to observe the damage they had been causing.' As Alan Rushton remarked, even if it was not possible to go on deck the air-vents could have been sealed below deck to prevent contamination from sea-water. The master was also criticized for the failure to use the anchor and for only sending a Pan Pan call when the Braer first got into trouble.

Like so many other captains in such circumstances, Gelis became something of a scapegoat although he was not in total charge. As Jonathan Wills points out: 'One of the problems with modern communications is that you can lift a phone on the bridge of a ship and you can talk to the office in New York and the office can lift their phone and call you, so there is much more possibility of people on shore interfering in the running of a ship. Traditionally, the captain was in charge. Nowadays, captains are under perhaps no greater pressures but they're under pressure more often because it's easier to get at them. They're no longer alone on the bridge. The captain has all sorts of people on shore, engineering superintendents, owners, managers, who can interfere with what he would once have regarded as his sole preserve. I suspect that somebody put undue influence on that captain. If they did, a crime has been committed – it's called barratry, the unauthorized interference with the conduct of a ship to the detriment of its cargo. Maybe that's what happened.'

Unfortunately, the inquiry into the disaster, headed by Lord Donaldson, was held in secret so the full story is not yet available. But, as Dickson points out, at least 'The safety zone around Shetland was increased from ten to twenty miles, which is fine, but unfortunately the government changed the wording on the chart that allows tankers in ballast into that area, which we are very strongly against. This safety zone should apply to both loaded and ballasted tankers, and we're still fighting that one tooth and nail.' And in a key section the report provided what Gordon Downard calls 'intervention powers, where if a vessel is reluctant to take towage, through our operational chain of command we can force her to do so.'

In July 1991, nature had again shown its capacity to clean up man-made disasters when the Greek tanker *Kirki* broke in two off the coast of Western Australia spilling 17,000 tons of oil in Australia's worst such disaster. The spill threatened the state's considerable crayfish industry as well as large colonies of sea-lions and seabirds. Nevertheless, a south-westerly wind carried the relatively light crude oil away from the coast and it soon broke up and evaporated, leaving virtually no trace on the shore.

The contrast between the relative environmental harmlessness of disasters like the *Kirki* and the *Braer* and the effects of the wreck of the *Sea Empress* in Milford Haven in western Wales three years later, showed the overwhelming importance of the location of a spill. The *Braer* lost her oil in stormy waters, ideal for reducing the impact. The *Sea Empress* ran aground in a landlocked estuary. The weather was fine and clear when a steering fault led her to ground on a rock in what was described as a 'saucer-shaped hole'.

This ensured that the rescue attempt was exceptionally difficult, even though some of the world's most powerful tugs were soon on the scene. The weather closed in, with westerly gales building up, before the tugs could turn the vessel round in the 'hole' and leave her with her bow facing the wind. For several days the tugs' crews fought to refloat the vessel but she kept bouncing back and forth on the rocks surrounding the 'hole'. In the end she was moved off her rock after six days – allowing six separate attempts to refloat her with the aid of twelve tugs – and the loss of over 70,000 tons of oil, creating a major environmental crisis in waters formerly famous for the richness of the marine life.

The *Sea Empress* disaster also contrasted with the story of the *Borga*, which had grounded in Milford Haven only three months earlier, also because of a steering error. She, too, took some time to refloat but, although the hull plates were damaged, she had a double hull and her cargo tanks remained intact: there was no pollution. Double-skinned hulls for tankers had already been made compulsory by the American government for any ships entering US waters, as a result of the *Exxon Valdez* disaster, while elsewhere in the world it is merely encouraged by insurance companies, which give a 15 per cent reduction in premium for any tanker with a double hull – and penalize older tankers. For the moment this has calmed environmentalists, though naval experts are worried that, in the long term, the space between the two skins of the hull will prove impossible to inspect and that the rusting inevitable with any ocean-going vessel will affect the tankers' strength. Nevertheless, it is an encouraging sign that action is being taken to reduce environmental dangers.

To reduce, not stop. For, as Steve McCall of the Valdez coastguard says, 'If you spill oil on water, it's not like spilling oil on your driveway. It is not going to sit there and wait while you get something to mop it up. When you spill oil on water you have a fluid on top of a fluid and they both move. They're both affected by currents, by wind, by tides. The oil is going to move and it's a moving target. You're always trying to catch and get ahead of it. And even though you have a lot of equipment and a lot of trained people and a lot of best efforts by people, if the elements are against you, the ultimate collection area for oil is going to be the shoreline.'

10
The Salt Smell of Scandal

Although the *Salem* took hours to sink, following a series of explosions, distress signals were not transmitted until another ship came in sight. And while some of the rescued crew carried packed suitcases and freshly cut sandwiches, for quite inexplicable reasons there was no time for the ship's log to be saved.

Eric Ellen*

One of the oldest (and most racist) of all the Jewish jokes that I grew up with, coming from a Jewish family in North London, relates how Hymie met Solly in the street. Hymie commiserates, 'I'm sorry to hear about the fire.' 'Shush,' replies Solly, 'it's not until tonight.' The idea of burning down an over-insured warehouse containing unsaleable goods is still known in some circles – Jewish and non-Jewish – as 'Jewish stocktaking'. In shipping circles the practice is known as 'rust-bucket fraud', mainly because the ships involved are usually barely seaworthy. In these instances, the story would be thought of as concerning two Greeks, since there has always been a steady flow of over-insured Greek ships that have gone down in the world's oceans. In this sense, Greece counts as the leading flag of convenience, under whose auspices most maritime frauds are committed.

This is no exaggeration. An analysis performed in the late 1970s by a leading underwriter of fifty-two cases of the non-delivery or misdelivery of cargo showed that all were registered in Cyprus, Liberia, Panama or Greece – the last of which accounting for nearly half the total. A similar analysis of fraud in general showed that, in 1979, there was an average of three a month, averaging about $1 million – which still excluded the vast

*International Maritime Fraud, Sweet & Maxwell, London, 1981, is the major source for the earlier sections of this chapter.

majority of such frauds that go unreported. Most of the ships involved were over fifteen years old, and half of the ninety-two were registered in Greece.

The frauds involve every type of malfeasance, from the forging of documents to the disappearance or misrouting of cargo – or ships. In most cases there is a Greek connection, even when the vessel involved is not Greek-registered. The reason is simple: the Greeks are ingenious, and they dominate the world of maritime trading. Moreover, they lack what might be described as civic consciousness, as well as the scruples that prevent less imaginative people from deceiving the authorities.

Eric Ellen and Donald Campbell[†] recount a typical case of fraud in which cargo is diverted while *en route* to its legitimate destination, then sold off as surplus, cut-price merchandise. This scam is particularly prevalent when the cargo consists of non-perishable consumer goods in handy sizes and where the destination is a Third-World country, which tends to insure the cargo itself and lacks the machinery for investigating fraud. As for the ship, Ellen says, she 'may cease to exist. She may end up on the seabed or continue under a new name and a new flag.'

All this and more was involved in the absurd, delightful and typical case of the 1,500 tons of canned tomato paste destined for Libya aboard the MV *Mariner*. She was registered in Piraeus and owned by two Greeks, both called Papaioannou. She set sail from a Greek port on 28 November 1977, a few days after being sold to a Panamanian company. On 3 December, two days after she should have arrived at the Libyan port of Tripoli, rumours began to circulate that the tomato paste was being offered for sale through brokers in Beirut. The shippers asked Interpol and anyone else they could think of to find out what was happening. They were not helped in their task by the ship's change of name – to *Arine*, *Aloha* and *Marina K*.

In mid-January, the Lloyd's agent at Guinea-Bissau in West Africa reported that a ship called the *Tarina T* had arrived and was discharging 110,000 tins of tomato paste. His efforts to trace what had happened to it were hindered by the local authorities. They said that Guinea-Bissau, a small enclave on the west coast of Africa between Senegal and Guinea, was effectively lawless and indeed lacked a proper legal system. As a result, only the government could initiate proceedings and then only in criminal cases.

† *op. cit.*

But they appointed a Miss Steflan to investigate. She spoke to the broker handling the paste but not to the Lloyd's agent and closed the case.

In the meantime the paste had been loaded on board a ship called, first, the *Gale*, which changed its name to *Daler* before unloading at the port of Conakry in Guinea-Bissau. At Conakry the Lloyd's agent showed the authorities the documents proving that the cargo belonged to the Libyans. By then the paste had been sold by a Geneva-based firm, Etablissement Guimabi to Olivier International, based in Lausanne ('At a very cheap price,' said Olivier's export manager, P. H. Kienberger), before being sold to the Guinean government's import agency. Kienberger tried to unravel the deal, but much of the paste was lost for ever, probably ending up in the stew-pots of West African families.

There are also, of course, many more elaborate frauds. The biggest concerned the *Salem*, a 213,000-ton Liberian tanker, allegedly full of oil from Kuwait, that went down off the coast of West Africa in January 1980. Fortunately the master and crew were saved.

The fraud, and the reason behind it, began to emerge quite quickly. There was considerable interest, if only because the *Salem* was so large: she was carrying nearly 200,000 tons of oil. Also, when she was built, in 1969 in Sweden, she was the most advanced ship ever produced. The insurance was high: $24 million for the ship and $60 million for the oil.

The disappearance can be traced back to the takeover of Iran by the Ayatollah Khomeini. Then Iran cut off supplies of oil to South Africa because its Jewish community was an important backer of Israel. The South African government had set up an oil-broking company called Haven International to buy supplies in the 'spot' market, that is, for immediate delivery.

Haven soon lived up – or down – to its name by attracting some shady characters. One was a Lebanese-born American life-insurance salesman called Fred Soudan, one of the three principal actors in the comedy-drama of the *Salem*. He arranged to buy the ship, then called *South Sun*, for $11.5 million claiming that he had come into an inheritance, although the money almost certainly came from a South African bank. To complete the transaction he used a Liberian company, Oxford Shipping, owned by two Greeks, Andrew Triandafilou and John Avgerinos.

Soudan then arranged for the *Salem* to be chartered to a Liberian concern, Shipomex, owned by a man known as Bert Stein, through a broker in Rotterdam called Anton Reidel. The *Salem*'s master was a Captain Dimitrios Georgoulis, who had worked his way up to be master of several ships, even though his only qualification was a chief mate's licence from the Republic of Panama. Later it emerged that he was already being investigated for the loss of the freighter *Alexandros K* while on her way from Bulgaria to Egypt with a cargo of steel bars. Like the *Salem*, she foundered, but not before her name had been changed to *Leila* and the cargo landed in the Lebanon. The owners of the *Alexandros K* owned another ship called the *Brilliant*, which went down in a sinking that bore some resemblance to that of the *Salem*: distress signals were fired only when rescue was close at hand. Indeed Georgoulis' passport had been confiscated by the Greek police because of the *Alexandros K*; he embarked on the *Salem* under the name of Jimmy Georgoulis, by using an American passport.

The *Salem* loaded 193,000 tons of oil in Kuwait and set sail, ostensibly for Italy. Halfway through the voyage the oil was bought by Shell in a typical transaction on the spot oil market. By 27 December the tanker, by now renamed *Lema*, was off Durban and discharged 173,000 tons of oil, taking on sea-water to give the impression that she was still carrying the original cargo and leaving in the tanks enough oil to form a slick after the sinking. Georgoulis went ashore and met officials from Haven, who assumed that the cargo from the *Lema* (ex-*Salem*) was merely the first of many. Even before the oil had been offloaded and paid for (to Reidel, who had flown to Johannesburg to receive the money) Triandafilou and Avgerinos had removed Soudan from the board of Oxford Shipping, and Soudan then sued them.

Meanwhile, life on the ocean wave had assumed a dramatic dimension. In the early morning of 16 January fire allegedly broke out on board the *Lema* while she was off the coast of Senegal. After a single explosion, captain and crew headed for the boats, allegedly fearing further explosions. Georgoulis claimed that he sent an SOS, though none was received. By 1030 a tanker, the British *Trident*, had picked up captain and crew.

Two Scotland Yard detectives were soon on the case and discovered that Georgoulis had stayed in a Durban hotel (with the wife of the ship's electrician whom he then sent back to Greece) where he had made a number of phone calls to Greece. The evidence of fraud piled up – helped by an admission from the South Africans that the *Lema/Salem* had indeed delivered oil to their country. By 4 August 1980 the British-based insurers had enough proof to go before City of London magistrates who issued warrants for the arrest of Soudan, Reidel, Georgoulis and Johannes Lock, 'also known as Bert Stein', on a variety of charges of fraud and conspiracy.

Soudan was duly brought to trial and sentenced to between three and five years imprisonment on charges of wire fraud, perjury, and tax irregularities. After serving only two-and-a-half years of his sentence he escaped and disappeared. The captain, the ship's agent and four of the ship's officers were all sentenced to long terms of imprisonment in their native Greece, but on appeal all these sentences were reduced. As for Triandafilou and Avgerinos, a Liberian court of inquiry recommended that they be detained, but they were freed by Master Sergeant Samuel Doe soon after he seized the reins of power in Liberia.

The single most important instance of maritime fraud – that I've come across – concerns the *Lucona*. In January 1977 this unremarkable freighter left the Italian port of Chiaggia ostensibly bound for Hong Kong. Three weeks later, she sank off the Maldive Islands in the Indian Ocean west of Sri Lanka, taking with her six of her crew and the uranium-processing plant that, allegedly, she had been carrying.

The disaster was merely the prelude to a scandal that rumbled on for a full fourteen years and struck at the heart of the Austrian establishment. During that time a leading minister in the government shot himself, another major figure in the country's political life was convicted of murder, and the Austrian public woke up to the corruption of its long-ruling Socialist party, largely due to the ramifications of the *Lucona* affair.

The anti-hero responsible for the upheaval was one Udo Proksch. Born in Rostock, Germany, in 1934, he had worked briefly as a swineherd and a miner before he made a fortune designing spectacles – using Vienna as a base for dabbling in deals with Eastern Europe. In 1970 the ebullient Proksch bought Demel's, the most celebrated pastry-shop in Vienna, a city which takes its confectionery, and therefore its confectioners, more seriously than anywhere else in the world. A back room was the home of Club 45, which he set up with two leading Socialist politicians, Leopold Gratz and Hannes Androsch, who would have become chancellor had it not been for accusations of dubious arrangements in building contracts. With that sort of backing, Club 45 soon numbered among its members most of the inner ring of the Socialist establishment.

In 1977 Proksch's company, Zapata, had chartered the *Lucona*, allegedly to transport 'uranium-processing machinery'. On leaving Italy the ship reached the Maldives in good time but was rocked by a mysterious explosion. The captain, Johann Puister, later testified that he had rushed up on to the bridge after seeing a mass of smoke from the middle of the ship and hearing 'a terrible groaning and hissing sound from the same direction'. He suspected that 'something in the cargo had exploded or, rather, erupted. Neither my wife nor the chief officer heard an explosion. The damage to the sides and/or bottom of the ship must have been enormous as the vessel sank in a minute or so. I observed no gas, nor heat, nor smell. Therefore it cannot have been the smoke of a fire.' He and most of the crew managed to clamber aboard a dinghy but six were lost.

Proksch had paid $100,000 to insure his 'precious' cargo for over $18 million with the Viennese insurance company Bundesländer, which had little experience of maritime insurance. When Zapata filed an insurance claim for $10 million the insurers smelt a rat and hired a German private investigator, Dietmar Guggenbichler, to find out more. They suspected that not only had the ship been deliberately scuttled, but also that there had never been any 'uranium-processing machinery' on board in the first place. But Guggenbichler was pilloried in the press amid claims that he had been hired by opposition political parties to discredit the Socialists.

The fraud had been long in preparation. In 1971 one of Proksch's companies, which he owned with Stephen Low, a Canadian adventurer and long-time associate, and Hans Peter Daimler, a German wheeler-dealer, had bought obsolete coal-mining plant and sent it to a factory near Vienna. There, amid elaborate security precautions he arranged for Italian labourers to polish and paint the machinery, and several tons of scrap iron. As the *Lucona* had sailed for Hong Kong, a sheaf of backdated customs and delivery documents had been prepared, probably with the help of the Romanian secret service with whom Proksch had had dealings in the past. Proksch had met a Swiss arms dealer and industrialist named Erwin Egger, who owned a company called Decobul, which appeared in the files of Proksch's company, Zapata – but not those of Decobul! – as owners of the uranium machinery.

When the insurance company refused to pay up, Proksch and Daimler sued. But within a few years the plot started to unravel. In 1981 Karl

Lutgendorf, the Austrian defence minister, who was himself a shareholder in Proksch's company, was found with the back of his head blown off. The official verdict on his death was suicide but doubts remained. In 1983 criminal investigations were launched against Proksch but were blocked by the minister of the interior and by his partner in Club 45, Leopold Gratz, by then the foreign minister. Gratz went so far as to produce a document purporting to show that the machinery had been delivered back in 1974 by a Romanian state company. (The document was later found to be a forgery, but by that time the prosecution had been abandoned.)

The breakthrough in the case was political. In the country's general election in 1986 Proksch's party, the Socialists, suffered a severe setback, which forced them to form a coalition government with the Conservatives, who had no interest in covering up the fraud. Moreover, an army explosives expert, Major Johan Edelmaier, confessed that he had supplied Proksch with 100 kilograms of explosives the year before the *Lucona* sank – arranged under cover of a training film made by Proksch and backed by the same defence minister who had apparently committed suicide so conveniently in 1981.

Another victim was Gratz, the former foreign minister who had been strongly tipped as the Socialist candidate in the 1986 presidential elections. But the scandal caught up with him, and a colourless candidate was nominated and defeated by Kurt Waldheim, the former secretary-general of the UN who, it later emerged, had served the Nazis so faithfully in Greece during the Second World War. The revelations of Waldheim's past came at much the same time as the Proksch affair, and revolutionized the standards of Austrian public life: 'Before Proksch and Waldheim it was not a sin to lie in Austria,' said one MP.

In 1986, interest in the case intensified with the publication of *The Lucona Case* – later the basis for a film directed by Jack Gold – which provided chapter and verse for the fraud. A parliamentary inquiry was launched, and Proksch and Daimler were prosecuted. Proksch virtually admitted his guilt by fleeing to the Philippines, which does not have an extradition treaty with the Austrians. There, he underwent plastic surgery to change his appearance, set up home with a faith-healer, and started to make pornographic movies. Foolishly, in 1989 he changed planes in Vienna *en route* for London and was arrested despite his attempts at disguise. Daimler was extradited to Germany.

Only then was a serious attempt made to find out what had actually happened. The experienced American firm Eastport International – which had already retrieved the crucial part of the booster rocket that had destroyed the space shuttle *Columbia* – was hired to find the wreck of the *Lucona* by the judge. He supervised the search to the north-west of Male in the Maldives, intent on ensuring that there was no further fraud. A sonar device hovering 1,200 feet above the ocean floor, which was over two miles deep, eventually located the *Lucona* almost exactly where the survivors had said it was. The search vessel, an ageing offshore supply ship, then launched a robot submarine to photograph it. The pictures showed a scene of utter devastation. Nothing remained of the ship except a length of its double-bottomed hull. 'It looked like someone just cut it [the top of the ship] with a blow torch,' said Bill Lawson, one of Eastport's specialists. The peculiar twisting of the plates of the hull suggested a huge explosion, which would have involved around a hundredweight of explosives loaded in an area of the ship where Proksch's 'uranium plant' had been stored. This clue led the investigators to believe that a time-bomb had been set to detonate while the ship was sailing in deep water. Moreover, the labels on the sixteen crates that had allegedly contained the 'uranium-processing machinery' proved that they held the collection of machinery and scrap assembled by Proksch and Daimler.

In 1991 Proksch was found guilty of murder and insurance fraud, and sentenced to twenty years' imprisonment. Before the *Lucona* had sailed on her last voyage the world's best-connected confectioner had delivered one of his fabled chocolate tortes as a farewell present to the crew. As the state prosecutor told the jury: 'The cake was not a travel provision, but the condemned's last meal, provided by the executioner.'

11
The Power of the Waves

We knew that it happened so fast nobody knew what had hit 'em and what was happening.
Dudley Paquette, captain of the Wilfred Sykes

The sinking of the bulk carrier *Edmond Fitzgerald* on Lake Superior on 10 November 1975 with the loss of twenty-nine lives was in one sense a demonstration of the apparently random nature of such tragic events, that they can occur in what seem like sheltered inland waters. It also demonstrates the typical multiple causes of a disaster and the difficulty of solving a complex series of problems to pinpoint the principal reason for a shipwreck. But the *Edmond Fitzgerald* is also something of a curiosity: it became the subject of a famous folk song by Gordon Lightfoot, which – like those celebrated nineteenth-century railway disasters, 'The Wreck of the Old 97' and 'The Cannonball Express', driven to its fate by Casey Jones – has ensured that the *Edmond Fitzgerald* has not been forgotten by the American public. Also, the case involved small communities in the Midwest of the United States not normally thought vulnerable to the vagaries of the sea. Last, but not least, the loss remains a mystery. Nevertheless, as Tom Holden, of the Army Corps of Engineers at the Lake Superior American Visitors' Center in Duluth, emphasizes, 'Without that ballad I don't know if we'd still be talking about it like we are today.'

Shipwrecks on Lake Superior, largest of the Great Lakes, are now infrequent. There have been 350 accidents in all, but the two before the *Edmond Fitzgerald* both occurred in 1953. 'That's one of the reasons,' says Holden, in the standard lecture he gives on the subject, 'why in 1975 it really took a little convincing for the coastguard to believed that the *Fitzgerald* had gone to the bottom.'

The excellent record is surprising, given the uncertainty of the weather.

On a fine day the Great Lakes are a beautiful sight – and as flat as a millpond. Yet Holden says, 'The lake changes every day. Even throughout the day you can watch it change. It can be quiet, we can have a breeze and hardly any waves at all or we can have very large waves, 12 to 15 feet high, even right at the harbour entry. It can be very dramatic where *Fitzgerald* sank, on the far eastern part of the lake. It's the nor-wester there that they have to worry about and it can be dramatic on that shore-line because as the wind drives the waves, the configuration of the lake shore allows those waves to bounce off and sometimes come back in two or three different directions. It can be really wild.'

Normally, says Dudley Paquette, the captain of the *Wilfred Sykes*, one of the boats that searched for the *Edmond Fitzgerald*, 'A low-pressure system will travel from south-west to north-east, and it worked right to the T on this storm of 10 November 1975. The Great Lakes has been described as a big suction cup that sucks these low-pressure systems right up because, maybe, of this vast amount of water in the five lakes and above in Hudson Bay.'

On 9 November the forecast was for such a system, with winds of up to 47 knots. The next day the *Edmond Fitzgerald* and her sister ship the *Arthur Anderson*, says Holden, 'had both loaded up at Two Harbors with the same kind of cargo, taconite pellets. The *Anderson* finished first and came out from Two Harbors. As they were leaving they got a report for the weather out on Lake Superior and essentially it was a storm on the far eastern edge, so the captain of the *Anderson*, Captain Cooper, decided to take the longer way across the lake, which would allow plenty of time for the storm to move, cross over the far part of the lake and get way up into Canada by the time the boats got over there. Then, a couple of hours later, as the *Edmond Fitzgerald* finished loading here in Superior and left the Burlington northern ore dock, they had a very similar weather report [and made] basically the same decision.' But when they had gone two-thirds of the way and had seen that the weather was going to be worse than forecast, 'They had to decide whether to continue going into the storm and go below Isle Royale, or to the north of Isle Royale to hide from the storm in some place up there in the water area of Thunder Bay.' In the event they continued south of Isle Royale, looking for the eye of the storm where conditions would not be so bad.

According to Captain Cooper of the *Arthur Anderson*, as reported by Holden, 'As they approached the eye of the storm they had winds 50, 60,

70 miles an hour, the waves were up around 25 feet or so, it was snowing heavily, it was heavily overcast. As they approached the eye of the storm, the snow dropped, the clouds parted, the sun came out, the waves dropped down to about 10 feet and the wind down to around 25 miles an hour. In that special little spot, right in the middle of the storm, he was able to turn the boat and head down the lake. Now the *Edmond Fitzgerald* had found the eye of the storm a little bit before the *Anderson* because she travelled ahead, so the two boats were now headed down Lake Superior [with the weather getting worse. With] the low pressure the wind goes backwards, it wants to run around counter-clockwise so now we had a following wind and following seas so the wind and waves are coming from the back of the boat. As that's happening there's getting to be more and more water up on the deck.'

At this point, according to Holden, there was apparently 'a radio call from the *Fitzgerald* back to the *Anderson*. Captain Macsaulcy, of the doomed boat, said that something had happened to the *Fitzgerald*. He mentioned three things. He said that he had a fence-rail down, he'd lost two ballast-tank vent-caps and he'd lost his radar. The fence-rail is usually two or three steel cables that run from one end of the boat to the other, right along the deck, just to keep you from accidentally stepping over the side.' He also said that the vent caps were missing from the two ballast tanks at the bottom of the boat. Remember, says Holden, 'the ballast tanks are supposed to be watertight compartments. But if water is being sucked out of one of those tanks, you need to allow air to get down in there to replace the water, so you need to have real loose covers – vent caps – on top.' However, these proved to be the weak spots in the ship's defences against the force of the waves.

'When he lost his radar, Captain Macsauley lost his ability to know exactly where he was on the lake. He asked Captain Cooper if he would shadow him down the lake. What he meant by that was that when he needed to know, would Captain Cooper tell him where he was and that they'd call each other probably about every half-hour. So we're heading for Caribou Island. Captain Cooper, who had been down below, came back up into the pilot-house. He looked at the radar screen and he commented to the first mate that he did not want the *Anderson* to pass as close to Caribou Island as the *Fitzgerald* had, so they changed course. There are a lot of reefs around Caribou Island and he didn't want to hit one. It wasn't long after that that they got another radio call from the *Fitzgerald*, this time to report that they had some damage and had developed a list.'

Macsauley reported that he was using the pumps but, 'more water was coming in than could be pumped out because the list had increased and weight is being added to the boat so she's sitting lower in the water. There are still those following winds and following waves, so more and more water is getting on the deck. This is now a wetter boat than it was originally designed to be for the cargo she was carrying. Around 26,000 gross tons of taconite was more cargo than she should have carried when she was brand new, and she'd been allowed to change her load-line or to carry more cargo twice in her career but each time not without having to do something to the boat. They knew that if you put in more cargo, the boat sits lower, and when the weather's bad there's going to be more water on the deck. In some cases they had to put stiffeners on the cabins to raise where the doorways are so the water couldn't just run into the boat. They also stiffened up the hatch-covers.'

According to the records, Captain Macsauley should have been well equipped for the crisis. He was not only a highly experienced sailor, with forty years' service, but he was also known as a 'weather captain', and had been in many of the major storms that autumn. So, says Holden in his lecture, the captain was thinking of the options – 'throwing in the towel and taking to the lifeboats, running the ship on the beach in Canada or keeping going. They elected to keep going. One of the reasons was that the other options weren't really good ones – remember, the lifeboats are at the back of the ship so in 25- or 30-foot seas only half the crew is anywhere near the lifeboats, and with the list, you could get only one lifeboat in the water, the one that was on the low side. It was big enough to hold everyone on board but half the crew was the length of the ship away, still in those huge waves, so my impression is that if they'd tried to abandon ship they probably would have lost half the crew, and by the time you've floated around in an open lifeboat, soaking wet, with the winds and temperatures they had, probably half of the people in the lifeboat would have died of hypothermia. So it was better to stay with the ship as long as the ship stuck with them – but the boat quit just a little bit early.' The master of the *Avafors*, a Swedish vessel also unlucky enough to be on the lake in the storm, received a call from the *Edmond Fitzgerald* explaining that she was now listing badly. Shortly afterwards there came the last call from the ship: 'We are holding our own.'

'Now, Captain Cooper was following the *Fitzgerald* on the radar,' continues Holden, 'and all of a sudden there was this little snow squall that passed between the two ships and the *Anderson* lost its radar signal. Then, as the screen started to clear, they could see the shoreline in Canada and other boats, but not the *Edmond Fitzgerald*.' Although apparently it took them half an hour to work out what had happened, the *Edmond Fitzgerald* had sunk during those crucial few minutes and it was soon clear that no one on board had survived.

By then the waves had subsided so the *Anderson* went back on to the lake together with other vessels, the *William Clay Ford*, the *Roger Blow* and Paquette's vessel the *Wilfred Sykes*, lining up a mile apart. They were looking for survivors, says Paquette. 'We found all the debris, life jackets, mattresses, half of a lifeboat, then an inflatable life-raft. There was nobody in it so we knew then that there were no survivors, not in those conditions. The water temperature was just above freezing and you couldn't have lasted a minute in it.'

The US Coastguard immediately set up an expert four-man committee to investigate the wreck, which lay in 500 feet of water near Chummy Bank next to Caribou Island. They were thorough, and interviewed everyone who could conceivably have helped their inquiries, from former members of the crew to the coastguards to the naval architect who had helped design the ship. According to Jim Wilson, a member of the committee, who at the time was in charge of the coastguard office in Detroit, 'After we had interviewed all the witnesses on our list and the two or three who came in and volunteered their services, we found that we didn't have enough information to make any concrete decisions. In the conference we had after that, the admiral said that we had no more witnesses to interview but I noted that we had missed one important witness and that was the hull of the vessel that lay on the bottom of Lake Superior. The decision was then made to videotape, photograph or otherwise observe it.'

Using an unmanned deep-diving module, the US Coastguard took nearly a thousand still photographs, recorded over 40,000 feet of videotape and undertook a sonic survey of the scene of the wreck. They found that while the stern was upside down, the bow section was the right way up – evidence that she had not capsized. Had she done so the two halves of the ship would have been the same way up. The underwater survey also showed that the hatch-covers over two of the holds were still intact. Had the ship turned over, they would have been ripped off by the weight of the cargo. The evidence also indicated that the ship had not broken up while still afloat.

Neither had she been overloaded. In fact, says Jim Wilson, 'There were two changes to the load-line since the *Fitzgerald* had come out, what she was originally assigned and then two incremental improvements, so at the time she sank she was able to carry about a third more cargo.'

The video camera also spotted that the cover of hatch number 5 had been ripped off. Some of the fastening 'dogs' were damaged, others open. Had they been done up properly they would either all have been ripped off or the hatch would have remained intact. This was proof enough that while the ship was struggling, low in the water, a wave had taken the cover off hatch number 5. The water flooded in and the ship soon went down, taking her crew with her. As Jim Wilson explains, 'When they went back to the original design for the ship [they found that the hatch-covers] could handle four feet of water just sitting on them, so in theory if we put five-foot waves on top of them maybe we could break one in, but with waves of up around 25 feet or so, we would have had enough water probably to break one of these hatch-covers. Later on it was found out that not only were these hatch-covers designed to withstand the weight of four feet of water, when they lowered the load-line, allowing the ship to take on more cargo, they also should have made those hatch-covers stronger and by a safety factor of about 425 per cent. We're talking not just handling four feet of water that there was originally, we're talking four and a quarter times that on top.

'The visual evidence we got indicated that approximately every sixth hatch clamp in the forward section of the vessel was damaged. That meant five out of six were undamaged.' But, still, this indicated 'that the clamps weren't doing their job, they were not holding the hatch-cover tight. That in turn meant that as the vessel worked in the seaway the hatch could flex, opening a gap where water could get into the hold, so we now knew that water could get into the hold through the ineffective hatch closures. The amount of water at this point was unknown but when we discounted the *Fitzgerald* breaking apart on the surface, when we discounted grounding, the only thing we were left with, water that would let enough get in to sink the vessel, was flooding topside. So we now knew that the basic cause was flooding from topside through ineffective hatch closures. The only thing unknown was how long the water had been entering.

('After the results of the board came out, we started hose testing Great Lakes vessels as a condition of their certification in the spring. We found that we were having problems with the hatch gaskets. We found that many vessels needed adjustment of the clamps. That was easy enough to do. Others needed renewal of the gaskets because they had deteriorated. That was not too difficult, either, but we found three vessels that, no matter what we did, the only solution to the problem was to replace those gaskets with heavier gaskets. As we looked into this further we found that five vessels were made with very thin hatch-cover gaskets. Three of these were the ones we had the problem with. A fourth was the *Arthur B. Homer*, in a shipyard in Duluth, and we hadn't tested it. In fact the *Homer* never sailed again, went to the scrapyard afterwards, and the fifth vessel was on the bottom of Lake Superior.')

Captain Cooper testified that the waves were amply big enough to crush the hatch-covers on the *Fitzgerald*, waves that, as Holden puts it, 'were 40 or 50 feet high. We had plenty of water on top of the hatch-covers to cave them in and once the hatch-covers are caved in, you've got enormous holes in the deck. With the hatch-covers off we can have tons and tons of water pour into the ship in the front part very fast. It noses into a wave, it doesn't have that buoyancy to come back up again and so it starts on the way to the bottom, and as it's sliding to the bottom the front going down is trying to raise the back of the boat up, and still as it's sliding it's trying to break the boat at a place that's moving all the time as it gets lower in the water. About two-thirds of the way back it seems that it snapped across the deck, the crack, which is the weakest part of the ship, but it didn't just snap like a dry twig, it broke more like a green stick, so it snapped across the deck, part way down the sides. Then it ripped forward and worked its way through the bottom.'

Wilson testifies that 'We know from the weather reports that as the vessel proceeded up the lake toward the Canadian lee [shore], she was taking seas on the port bow of the vessel. These seas were boarding the vessel. We know from the underwater photographs that the hatch clamps were not tight, which meant there were some gaps. The gaps meant that water could enter into the cargo hold. If the water entered in evenly then the vessel would sink bodily due to the amount of added weight. If it didn't enter in equally, then one side or the other would develop a list because the taconite pellets absorb water like a sponge. As more water went in, the list would become greater and greater. If the list got to eight degrees, the deck edge would be under water. We don't know what Captain Macsauley's comment about his fence being down really meant. Did it mean that it was physically broken, or did it mean that it was down in the water because of the list? Either one of those could have been true because neither one was ever explained by Captain Macsauley nor asked by Captain Cooper.'

Nevertheless, as Tom Holden says, no one really believes the hatch-cover theory. 'History says that no one had a problem with hatch clamps before the *Fitzgerald* and no one has had a problem since, so this may have been the exception, but maybe there was something else. I think that, yes, the hatch-covers had a lot to do with it but I think a series of events led up to the catastrophic finish and that a big part of that was shoaling in my mind. I think she passed close enough to Caribou Island to strike the shoals in that area, on Chummy Bank, and that would allow water into the ballast tanks in the bottom of the boat and account for the list. Without accounting for that list I don't think we have a solid theory.

'It became a vessel with a list and, in fact, a slowly sinking ship. Toward the end, very large rogue waves out on the lake were a big factor. Captain Cooper said that the *Anderson* was hit by two very large waves. If they had continued at the same speed, in the same direction that they were going, they would have reached the *Fitzgerald* at about the same time as that little snow squall blotted out the *Fitzgerald*'s image on the *Anderson* radar. Those two waves certainly would have been large enough to cave in the number 1 and number 2 hatch-covers right behind the pilot-house. When you've got a hole as large as one hatch opening and then two tons of water pour into a vessel very quickly, it would nose into a wave and not have the buoyancy to come back up again. I think that what started the sinking was hatch-cover failure but due to large boarding seas.' He believed that the hatch covers did indeed fail but only because if the increased pressure caused by the grounding and the subsequent list.

If Holden is right, then the shoals must have been more extensive than had been thought. This is perfectly possible. He looked at 'a map like they were using in 1975 and then at a map from about six or seven years later of this space around Caribou Island. We found a couple of things. One is that some shoals actually moved and the other was that the area marked dangerous got larger, so over time they found some more shoals in this general area that they didn't know about in 1975. In the area around Caribou Island where the *Fitzgerald* passed, she could have damaged herself and ended up with water in the ballast tanks that caused the list.'

In storm conditions, the shallower the water the rougher the sea. The master of the *Arthur Anderson* believed that the *Edmond Fitzgerald* had strayed into shallow water. In a telephone conversation with the two ships' operators, Macsauley had mentioned that the *Edmond Fitzgerald* had 'passed right over the six-fathom spot'. It is possible that the damage sustained at this point triggered a progressive disintegrating with the ship 'labouring, pitching and rolling' to her doom.

Jim Wilson flatly disagrees with the grounding theory. When the coastguard found the upturned after-third of the vessel, 'The bottom was visible to us throughout and we found there was no damage on the bottom except where the separation was and in a couple of small buckles, but no indentations, no tearing into the tanks. Then we knew that any damage, if there was any, from a grounding had to happen in the forward two-thirds of the vessel.' He's simply not convinced that the *Fitzgerald* actually hit Chummy Bank at all. 'Even if she came close to Chummy Bank,' he says, 'the question was, would she tear her bottom out? If she did damage to the bottom and the water only came into the double bottoms, then the vessel can make Whitefish Bay. If she tears into the cargo hold the vessel sinks rapidly because she has no sub-division. If she went aground off Caribou you'd have found her off Caribou. The indication that she was close to Chummy Bank came from a questionable range and bearing given by *Anderson*. Grounding didn't make sense as the only cause of loss of the vessel. That left us with the break-apart on the surface and we knew that didn't fit. When we found the hatches and the hatch clamps that were undamaged, we suddenly realized that we had been looking in the wrong direction. We then started looking at the hatch clamps and we did the calculations to show that damage to them would sink the vessel.'

Apart from grounding and hatch clamps, a third theory has been put forward by Paquette, that the ship broke its back, an accident caused by metal fatigue in the hull, and that, moreover, Captain Macsauley had thought something was wrong. 'He was on his last trip,' says Paquette, 'and he was going to return to the shipyard for the winter to undergo repairs. A ship that size normally wouldn't lay up and finishing the season in the middle of November. I proceeded until 20 January so there was an indication that there was something wrong.'

Paquette's theory is that 'The ship is bending, flexing, and if you take a piece of metal and bend it like that throughout a lifespan of seventeen years, something's going to break eventually. Two years later I was promoted to our flagship. She was a foot longer than the *Edmond Fitzgerald* and we did crack there. We tied the ship up at the dock and were going down the dock when water started coming out of where the rivets were in the crack in the plate. She broke exactly on the hinge and she broke on both sides. We had to stop loading, go over to the shipyard, dock her and replace and repair that whole section we call the hinge.'

His colleague Gerry Lawson was in the dock 'with the chief engineer when we saw the water coming out. I was amazed at how deeply into her internal structure she was cracked – 15 to 18 feet in. It was a major fracture about one-third forward on the port side. There was a vertical crack in the ship's side and the ballast water was just pouring out through it.'

'My professional opinion,' says Paquette, 'is that the *Fitzgerald* broke and cracked on the hinge, and the flagship, which is only a foot longer, cracked in the same spot' – the hinge, about two-thirds to the back of the ship at the point at which the stern section begins. 'Luckily for us, on this particular ship, it was July, we had nice weather. It could have happened out where the *Fitzgerald* was. Who knows?'

But Wilson scorns the idea of the *Fitzgerald* breaking up on the surface for two reasons. 'First, the two sections that we found were close together. If the ship had broken apart on the surface the two sections would have been found further apart. The last vessel that broke on the surface in Lake Huron, the *Daniel J. Morrell*, the bow section and the stern section were five miles apart. The second thing was, when we looked at all the breaks that we could see, and the primary one was the fracture of the after-section, all we found was ductile tearing, no brittle fracture. A break on the surface would have implied that it had a brittle fracture.'

That's not the final mystery. Logs of radar readings from the *Anderson* during the crucial period while she was guiding the *Edmond Fitzgerald* are missing, and there are suspicions that the conversations between the *Anderson*'s master and his bosses ashore were somehow tampered with. In the end the *Edmond Fitzgerald* took its secrets with it – a melancholy fact, which makes it an even more suitable subject for a ballad.

12
When Death was a Racing Certainty

We were an organized boat in a disorganized storm
Participant in the 1979 Fastnet Race

The 1979 Fastnet race, which proved fatal for fifteen unlucky participants, is a classic case of what is called in the air-safety establishment 'tombstone technology', belated action which is possible only after a well-publicized tragedy. It also helped to transform ocean-yacht racing from a weekend sport to a serious business. The race itself is one of the most glamorous in the yachting season, held every two years since 1925. The yachts sail from Cowes on the Isle of Wight round the Fastnet Rock off the south coast of Ireland and back to Plymouth, a distance of just over six hundred miles. Until 1979 it had proved remarkably safe, with only one death recorded in 1931 when one man had been swept overboard.

Alan Green* explains that: 'In 1925, the Fastnet race had less than a dozen boats but in 1979 there were 305.' One of the most unusual aspects of the race was the wide variation in the size of the yachts involved, which ranged from 28 feet to 85 feet in length. In 1979 this variation proved fatal. 'We started the race at Cowes in the usual way and everything seemed to be absolutely normal, no particular problems. The weather wasn't unduly severe, we weren't aware of any difficulty with the forecast.'

The race started on a Saturday and by Monday the organizers had moved to the finish. Green recalls: 'As I was on the finishing line at Plymouth at the lighthouse on the breakwater, news began to come in that all was not well. We learned quickly that extremely severe weather had hit the fleet and caused a great deal of trouble.' The reason, says John Rousmanière,† 'was

*Alan Green was secretary of the Royal Ocean Yacht Club at the time of the 1979 Fastnet race. He is now director of racing and special events.
†Author of *Fastnet Storm Force 10* Nautical Publishing Company, London, 1983.

a very unusual storm for mid-August in England, anywhere. It was essentially a winter storm. We traced it back to the Mid-west. A cell developed in the very hot plains, cold air was fed into it from the north and it made its way across New York. It blew down a toll booth on a turnpike in New Jersey, it came across Connecticut, it hit a fleet of racing boats in Newport and capsized some of them. Then it went up the New England coast and disappeared off the coast of Maine. Once it was in the Atlantic it almost died, but another storm had been through just a day or two beforehand and that had warmed up the water. [This] re-energized the storm and it drove across the Atlantic. And this is where it disappeared. In those days, before sophisticated satellite weather systems of the kind that are familiar to us today, storms were identified largely by ships at sea and by aeroplanes. And they missed it. Then, suddenly, it appeared as a cell, and it worked its way almost directly to where the fleet was going to be. It deepened as it came across, it was highly unstable, but there seemed to be almost . . . a dramatist might say there was a sense of purpose about it, that it was aimed at this fleet. And when it hit, it had this energy of shifty winds and lots and lots of little pieces of low-pressure systems. After it blew across us, I had a friend who was in Wales at the time, where a five-hundred-year-old wall was blown down by the storm. It went across Scotland, cancelled a ferry-boat service across the Channel for two days and then finally died out, off Norway. You could trace it almost in a straight line as it worked its way from Minnesota to Scandinavia.'

The storm hit the fleet more quickly than the forecasters had predicted, bringing with it waves of over 40 feet, thanks to gales that seemed to arrive from several directions at once. By 0300 the next morning a number of Mayday signals had been reported, and by first light a whole armada of ships, aircraft and helicopters had been mobilized, including four lifeboats and a Nimrod aircraft, which acted as a flying command post. In the event lifeboats from thirteen stations were called out, some several times. Nine towed yachts to safety and nine escorted yachts into harbour, while the helicopters brought in seventy-four people, of whom three were already dead. Fortunately, says Green, 'The rescue services in that part of the world were probably as good or better than anywhere else, the RAF, the coastguard, the Navy. The Dutch navy was already present because they had generously decided to send an escort ship, not particularly for safety purposes but to show the flag.

'So the main purpose of our headquarters, which was run by me, was communications. Three hundred and five boats, many different nationalities of crew, so one of the first phenomena that we found was that all the telephone lines in Plymouth were swamped. People with relatives in the race, from everywhere, from Australia, from the USA, you name it, they were all trying to telephone. This was in the days before teletext and the Internet, if you can think back that far, so the means of communication, compared with what we have now, were quite limited. Our job was to co-ordinate the information flow. The coastguards needed to know who'd been rescued, who'd arrived and so on. The rescue services needed to know who was still out there, and we really held the key database.'

The yacht *Grimalkin* was having a particularly hard time. The owner's son, Matthew Sheahan, explains how although it was their first Fastnet race 'we'd done a lot of offshore miles before that to get up to speed. Obviously, the Fastnet is something that people set their sights on and work up to. It's not something you jump into and have a quick go at. You certainly can't now.' Even when the weather turned rough they weren't too worried. As Matthew says, his father 'was a very methodical man who left nothing to chance. All the watch systems were detailed out, we had more safety gear than you could throw a stick at and everything had been planned for.'

They put on their safety harnesses and thought they were ready for the worst. At first they had no problems. Then it got dark. 'We'd reduced sail right down to absolutely nothing' says Matthew. 'We were just sailing under bare poles and still having trouble slowing the boat down, trying to keep it from being knocked down. We were looking at wind speeds of probably in excess of 50 knots but it wasn't so much the wind. The big problem was that the wind had actually swung through something like 90 degrees, which had set up another set of big, steep waves that were coming in at an angle to the others and the interaction between the two made the seas almost impossible to get through. We're talking about huge waves that were conservatively estimated at an average height of say 40 foot – some of the rogue waves could have been up to twice that height. It's looking at waves of 80 feet and pretty vertical – you know, like blocks of flats coming down on you, and it was just incredible to try to steer your way through it, in the dark as well.'

They had no idea where these waves were coming from. 'You could certainly hear them, the thunderous roar was just unbelievable as the top would break off and then gather pace as it sort of rolled down the face of the wave, and you could hear it coming. And perhaps one of the most frightening bits of it was actually hearing this horrendous noise and not quite knowing where it was coming from until it hit you.'

John Rousmanière was on a friend's yacht, the *Toscana*. He describes how on the Monday night 'The wind just started blowing harder and harder and harder, and in a series of very strong gusts gradually veering around into the west . . . As it came up, the seas got larger and larger and larger. It was impossible to hear, it was one of the noisiest nights I've ever spent in my life. With the roar, communications back and forth around the deck were extremely difficult. We had the roar of the water, water on deck, sometimes filling the cockpit. We had the wind howling into the fifties and sixties [m.p.h.]. And the boat became harder and harder to steer. The breeze just never settled down. If it had, the boat would have been easier to handle, because the seas would have had time to lengthen. But because of this constant rising and shifting of the wind, the seas were irregular.

'The good thing was it wasn't the first day, it was the third, so everybody was pretty much settled into the routine. The bad news was that it hit at night, which meant that it was completely dark except for these white rollers coming at you. And our bow-lights would reflect off the white rollers and you would have this eerie green and red reflected back at you by these white caps, smashing the seas. But you have very little sense of security when you're sailing at night in heavy weather. Your sense of sight to a great extent is turned off, which means that your other senses are heightened – hearing, for example, and the sound of those seas and that wind, it was like standing in a tube tunnel or a subway tunnel and hearing the train rocketing at you.

'What's the physical experience of going through conditions like this? Very tiring for everybody. Let's start with below, people trying to sleep. Unless you wedge yourself in with sea-bags, cushions and pillows, you're going to be sliding all over your bunk, even a very narrow sea-berth, except in a big heavy boat like ours, which was fairly stable amidships, if you're sitting up below, say you're the navigator, you would have to hang on at all times. Up on deck, if you weren't steering and didn't have anything to hold on to, you'd grab a lifeline or a winch and try to hang on. We had our safety harnesses on, so we were clipped on to the boat, and you could tighten the safety harness and that would give you a little security. But moving around on deck was difficult and most of the time you'd get on your knees and crawl if you were trying to get around in those conditions. At the helm, two hands are quite busy holding something moving rapidly. So you brace your leg to leeward and try to lean on that leg and try not to be thrown. But the boat is constantly going up and down and sideways, rolling, pitching, yawing, all at the same time. There's no experience ashore that's anything like it.'

At least *Toscana* was a substantial yacht. On the much smaller *Grimalkin* the crew kept getting knocked down and thrown into the water. The first time, they all bobbed up. Matthew's first reaction was, 'My God, that'll be something to talk about in the bar when we get back! I didn't realize at that stage that we were going to have enough knock-downs to see us into double figures.'

After the last capsize Matthew could see the boat upside down and, as he says, 'It's not quite the view you expect in the middle of the Irish Sea. I remember being shocked by that and thinking, This really is serious.' He managed to extricate himself from his safety harness which was just as well because the boat righted itself and if he had not he would have been dragged underneath. On the fifth knock-down Nick Ward, one of the crew, injured his leg badly, then *Grimalkin* was knocked down again, and David, Matthew's father, was trapped under the cockpit. To free him, the crew cut his safety harness. Two minutes later when the boat righted itself he drifted away and was never seen again. Nick Ward collapsed unconscious and Gerry Winks rolled, also unconscious, on top of him. When the boat overturned again Ward regained consciousness. Eight hours later a helicopter winched him off, with the body of Gerry Winks.

By then *Grimalkin* had lost two of its five crew members, and Matthew's father. Even getting into a life-raft seemed pointless: 'It's a bit like sitting in a paddling pool in the middle of a huge sea. It's only a small inflatable device and we were spinning down the faces of these waves like some outrageous fairground ride.' Unfortunately it was life-rafts the rescuers were looking for and, moreover, they'd been told that *Grimalkin* was miles away from its actual position. But at last they were spotted in a life-raft by a Hercules helicopter and picked up.

'The next thing that happens is quite amazing. This guy was winched down out of the helicopter then swam over, in these huge seas, to the life-raft. He stuck his arm over the edge and said, "All right then, lads, who's first?" and I thought, This is ridiculous. We're scared out of our wits here and this guy's swimming along as if it's just another job. Quite incredible.'

Of course, Matthew's first reaction was grief at the loss of his father, who was also his good friend. In the longer run 'It's made me believe in human nature, when you think, Christ, how could people ever cope with that? But people do. And it changed my attitude and made me feel that perhaps some of the slightly more petty things that I'd worry about on a day-to-day basis really were exactly that, just petty things.'

Another yacht, the *Ariadne*, was also rolled right over. Rob Robie, an American crew member, was washed away, probably because his safety harness snapped. Afterwards he was glimpsed once, fifty yards from the boat. At that point the remaining crew members decided to abandon ship. Two hours later a German freighter manoeuvred alongside. The life-raft had capsized but they managed to right it. Bob Gilders jumped for the rope-ladder hanging over the side and climbed to safety. Hal Feris jumped for the bottom rung but missed and was swept away. David Crisp climbed up the ladder but forgot to unhook himself from the dinghy. He was pulled back into the sea under the stern of the ship and never seen again. As a result there were only two survivors, Gilders and Matthew Hunt, from a crew of six (including the captain).

At the time it seemed natural to rely on a life-raft. 'I think you expect a life-raft to be just that,' says Matthew. 'You are safe in it. It's your last-ditch attempt to get safe. You give up the boat, you give up everything, but you maintain your life by getting into the life-raft, but it didn't prove to be the case for a lot of people. We didn't have as many problems as some people did. A lot of people found that their rafts didn't inflate properly or broke free from the lanyard that secured them to the boat. Ours inflated properly, we got into it, but it turned upside down.'

As John Rousmanière points out, 'The two great stories in England of seafaring in the 1970s were of people who had got into lifeboats, life-rafts and dinghies after their boats had been sunk by whales off the coast of South America, and survived in those boats and life-rafts for weeks at a time, and were picked up. Dougal Robertson and his family wrote a book about one of these incidents called *Survive the Savage Sea*, which was about just this. And that's what life-rafts are for, to save your life. I knew nobody who had been killed by a life-raft. They'd drowned on boats, but they hadn't been drowned in a life-raft. So they abandoned their boats, thinking that the boats were sinking. They had been rolled over, were full of water, the hatches had blown off, water had poured down through companionways, gear was flying all over the place, people had bad head injuries. But one thing they knew, from stories and experience and what they'd always been told, was that a life-raft was there to save your life. So they got into the life-rafts. In some cases the boats themselves survived. It led to a new rule: never get into a life-raft until you have to step up from the water into it. But they stepped down because they thought their boats were sinking. In one case, unfortunately, the two rings of the life-raft came apart, inflatable rings, and I think two men drowned as a result.'

The official report said that nearly half the yachts were knocked down to horizontal and a third, reported a knock-down that went further than the horizontal, including many complete roll-overs. But there was a wide variation in the experience of the different sizes of yachts. Of the fourteen larger yachts (those over 55 feet in length) that entered the race, thirteen finished and the other retired. Of the thirty-six boats between 44 and 55 feet long, sixteen finished, nineteen retired and one was abandoned. Lives were lost only in boats of below 39 feet, and the worst results came from the smallest. Of the 55 of between 28 and 33 feet, only one finished, 45 retired, seven were abandoned and two were sunk. In all, out of a record number of 305 entrants, 194 – nearly two-thirds – retired, nineteen were abandoned and five were sunk.

The event was an object lesson in survival as much as in sailing prowess. The winning yacht, *Tenacious*, was knocked down five or six times but as its skipper, the American media tycoon Ted Turner, put it: 'It was rough, but we had a good crew and a good big boat. I felt a little like Noah. I knew that the flood was coming and I had a boat ready that would get me through it.' In his pre-media tycoon days, Turner had already sailed five or six times in the Fastnet and was in one of the bigger boats. 'It was eight or ten years old,' he explains, 'which meant that it was more heavily constructed and engineered than a lot of the boats that were more modern and were out there in that storm.' Even he was a trifle daunted by the weather: 'Yes, I thought about stopping, for about thirty seconds. But I had raced over fifty thousand miles at sea, and the Fastnet Race of '79 was one of my last races. I'd had a very great amount of experience – I'd raced across the Atlantic twice, across the Pacific from Australia to New Zealand. I had done a lot of races and I had been in a lot of bad storms, and I knew I had one of the strongest boats out there.'

Not surprisingly, the tragedies induced some heart-searching among the racing community. A joint questionnaire was sent out by the Royal

Yachting Association (RYA) and the Royal Ocean Racing Club (RORC), which produced an overwhelming response. The most obvious finding, says Alan Green, confirmed sea-going lore – 'Don't leave your yacht until it actually sinks beneath you – because many who took to life-rafts found themselves in worse trouble. The yachts were later discovered, perhaps partly awash but still afloat, and would have been a better haven for the people than the rafts.'

The questionnaire also revealed a lack of basic seamanship which 'dictates that one should fix down all heavy objects. And it's just surprising how many people go to sea and don't do it . . . So we introduced rules whereby everything has to be fixed down and capable of withstanding a complete inversion. The worst offenders, perhaps the heaviest things in most boats, are batteries. In a sailing yacht the batteries are bigger than car batteries, more like lorry batteries, extremely heavy, and practically impossible for one person to lift on their own. If you imagine a piece of equipment like that breaking free or sliding out of its housing, which if it wasn't restrained it would do, the damage it would cause is substantial when a boat is on its side, or at a bigger angle, – and so is the injury. Even small objects, of course, would fly about in heavy weather. A can of baked beans will become a lethal missile – it can fly across the cabin and hit you on the head and you come off worst.'

According to John Rousmanière, the replies to the RORC's survey gave a 'very clear picture of how modern boats behaved in extremely difficult survival conditions. And they found that seventy-seven boats had turned upside down and many more had rolled over on their side, which no one would ever have dreamed would happen to an average family cruising boat. Even granting that this was an exceptional storm, there was probably something wrong with the design. So people here and in England did tests on computers and in test tanks and quite a lot of thinking about what it is that makes boats capsize. And it turned out that the trend in yacht design that had developed in the 1960s and 1970s, towards wider, lighter, shallower boats, tended to produce boats that did not have high ranges of positive stability – the degree to which a boat can heel, at which she stops heeling. How far will she go over before her keel and her design stop her from going over any more [and she rights herself]? When a mast is in the water, the positive-stability angle is about 100 degrees. What they want for offshore sailing is a boat that can be knocked down 120 degrees with the mast just

150

under water, which is pretty far, that'll pop back up again.'

Traditional boats were narrow and had heavy iron or lead keels. 'If you put a boat like that on its side,' says Green, 'the huge weight of the keel would give a very powerful re-righting movement. By 1979 the boats were much wider and shallower and designers had begun to discover that they could get better speed and racing performance by bringing the weight from the bottom of the keel up more, even into the canoe body of the hull, so that the keel would become more like a dinghy centreboard. Now you can see that the weight of the ballast is in a much less favourable position, so instead of being several feet away down below, as the boat goes on its side, that weight is in a far less powerful position to right the boat. Now, these effects had happened subtly and I think it's fair to say that none of us had really appreciated the safety implications. We were enjoying the faster, lighter boats, and they seemed thoroughly seaworthy. But they weren't. There was much less resistance to their turning turtle.'

These new-style boats, says Rousmanière, 'had ranges of positive stability of about 100 degrees, or 90 degrees, so they would go over to 100 degrees and they'd keep going. There was nothing to pull them back upright. And that's because of the beam, the shape of the hull, and because the keel was relatively light. And this is what they found in many of these smaller boats that went over in the Fastnet.' The result was a series of simple but scientifically calculated guidelines to help boat buyers.

Another problem, says Green, was that 'If you're sailing in heavy weather, you always like to have fresh air below which means you have to have a hatch open. Usually the one left open is the main hatchway, which leads down into the accommodation from the after-cockpit. And the way that hatchway is closed, typically, is by what you call the washboard, a kind of vertical shutter. It's very often a piece of flat, heavy timber, which slots into slides, and which is usually lifted out, even in very heavy weather. There's little risk of any water ever coming in there. The way that water usually gets into boats is over the bows.'

In 1979 many people were racing without the washboards in place. That meant, says Green, 'that the boat was really vulnerable, although many people failed to realize that. When a wave comes over the stern, and rolls forward, it can contain tons of water, literally tons. If you think of the size of an ordinary family car, it weighs a couple of tons. If you fill it with water you've probably got four or five tons of water there. That is significant. That amount of water in those conditions, with seas that were haphazardly tumbling over the back of the boat, rolling forward, finding an aperture perhaps the width of an ordinary doorway and a foot or so high – imagine the tons of water that can pour through into the interior in a very short time. We said that you must have the washboard fastened in by a lanyard, a strong piece of line, so if it gets pushed out of position it can be put back.'

Astonishingly, says Green, in Fastnet '79 'There were very few two-way radios on board, which sounds incredible now when we're about to have them on our wristwatches. After '79, we decided that we should make it mandatory. Maritime VHF for small boats was only just becoming available at a reasonable cost so it was introduced.' Previously, he says, they had been afraid that if too many such features had been introduced the participants would have raced in other contests where the conditions were less stringent.

Safety harnesses were also improved, as were life-rafts. Tests, says Green, 'really bore out what happened in the Fastnet '79: the life-rafts would tend to tip over fairly easily. Two main things were discovered to effectively prevent that. One was the installation of much bigger ballast pockets under the raft to improve stability. The other is the fundamental importance of a drogue or sea anchor, which plays almost a 100 per cent role in preventing capsizes. As a huge wave comes up to a craft it will tend to lift the craft and roll it over. If the craft is restrained by a line going up-wind then, amazingly, that line can hold the craft steady so that the turning moment of the wave underneath it passes beneath the craft and the craft doesn't roll over.' Better drogues are now mandatory.

The inquiry also tackled the question of size. Green admits that 'generally speaking, the larger the craft, the better it will survive heavy weather. But there are, of course, exceptions. We had in the Fastnet '79 boats between 32 feet overall length going right up to nearly 80 feet. The very large boats didn't get into trouble. That was, perhaps, for two reasons, though. One was that by and large they were fast enough to have got out of the worst conditions. The other was sheer size and it's a well-known fact in boat design that size brings its own safety factor. However, one of the 32-foot boats, *Contessa Thirty-two*, a beautiful, traditionally designed, strong little boat, finished the race without any real damage or difficulty. The crew just stuck it out and came through it perfectly well. So, although size is a factor, it doesn't necessarily mean that a small boat cannot survive.'

The new rules devised by the RORC were of enormous importance, since they were followed by over 30,000 yachts throughout the world and ensured that crews had to have greater experience before they could enter ocean races. But increased safety has also been helped by technical developments: air-sea rescue is easier, partly because of global-positioning systems, which give a precise idea of the position of even the smallest yacht. Fastnet '79 also led to the introduction of new, stronger materials, like carbon fibre for masts and rudders. Less obvious changes include more suitable clothing. 'For example,' says John Rousmanière, 'synthetic warm clothing that works even when it's wet has substantially replaced wool clothing in the last twenty years.'

Even more important was a transformation in attitudes. 'One of the lessons that came out of Fastnet, notes Rousmanière, is that Americans finally started to talk about safety as a serious concern on boats. There'd always been, there still is, a bit of a macho attitude about sailing and you see it in a variety of ways. People will run around on deck without shoes, stubbing their toes, blood all over the place. People don't wear foul-weather gear or sweaters when they're cold because *real* men don't get cold. Or you don't wear a life jacket, because *real* men never fall overboard or need a safety-harness to keep them from falling overboard or anything to keep them afloat when they go in the water. One of the effects of Fastnet and stories about it was to tell people that real men were out there and made those mistakes and drowned. Even so in June 1998 Eric Tabarly, greatest of all single-handed sailors, fell out of his beloved *Pen Duick 1* and drowned because he had not fitted a safety-harness.

'So we started to talk about safety in a public way, we started to have open seminars. I've run some in which we had six or eight hundred people turn up, to hear people talk about just the sort of thing we're talking about now, what kind of clothing to wear, what kind of skills to use, how to plan ahead. One of the most interesting things that I've noticed is that almost half of the people who come are women, and we're told that very often they drag their husbands along as well. Men don't really want to think seriously about that safety factor, but many women do, around boats. And I think that's led to a pretty substantial change of attitude.

'But yachting magazines over here [in the United States] didn't like to talk about safety. Boat-builders didn't want it known that their boats could sink or capsize, they didn't want it publicized. And the magazines thought this was negative editorial material. But in covering Fastnet and the follow-ups to that, I think they've gradually come around to taking boating safety a little more seriously.'

Another psychological change was the attitude to leadership. 'When a crew falls apart,' says Rousmanière, 'I've noticed that it's almost like losing your commander in a foxhole in the war. Morale falls apart, discipline collapses, the chain of command doesn't exist, people start making decisions on their own that might be good for the short-term but not for the long-term. People panic and, the worst thing, they stop making decisions. And, in the Fastnet, there were two or three boats in which the skipper was washed overboard, incapacitated or injured. And when that happened, the crew organization fell apart at just the time when they needed some decisiveness and leadership. And it's very hard to say this with an activity like sailing because we do it for fun. It isn't business, or the military, people go out there for enjoyment. It's very difficult – but it's important – to tell them that you have to organize yourselves so that there's a structure that allows others to fill in if the skipper, God forbid, is injured or becomes ill or is down below taking a nap.

'But I think the story of Fastnet and the many boats that got into such serious trouble has offered us an immense database to tell us that this is what happens when things fall apart on a boat. And among the lessons to be learned is how to select and organize your crew, the decisions you make when your life and the boat are at stake, how to balance all those priorities in some way.'

However, there's one problem that not even Rousmanière and the RORC can solve: experience. Ted Turner asks simply: 'How will crews get experience if they don't go out there? I think at the end of the day it's a matter of individual responsibility, but the only way you can get experience is to go out. Even with everything, that storm was a once-in-fifty-years storm, or something of that magnitude. And sailing's still probably safer than driving, you know. As unsafe as it is, it's still relatively safe.'

But perhaps the greatest lesson, in the words of the official report, is that 'The sea showed that it can be a deadly enemy and that those who go to sea for pleasure must do so in the full knowledge that they may encounter dangers of the highest order.' Of course, that's not going to deter true yachtsmen. As Ted Turner says: 'It's mainly a sport for masochists, really. Ocean racing is cold and wet, no women, no showers, just a minimum amount of food, if you're lucky, freezing cold. It's like climbing mountains like Mount Everest. There are people who like to test themselves against the elements, you know, like the people who want to ride a bike across Europe. It's people testing themselves. Maybe it's because most of us are just on the verge of madness.'

13
Hanging on in There:
the Art of Survival and Rescue

John Mortimer once asked a grizzled old mariner whether yachting was a dangerous sport. 'Not dangerous at all, provided you don't learn to swim,' he replied. 'When you're in a spot of trouble, if you can swim you try to strike out for the shore. You invariably drown. As I can't swim I cling to the wreckage and they send a helicopter out for me.'

Today, increasingly sophisticated systems for detecting ships, life-rafts, even human bodies in the water can give hope in situations that, until relatively recently, would have been hopeless. But even today it is still chance, rather than science, that has led to some remarkable rescues, such as when the *Berge Istra*, a 227,000-ton oil/bulk carrier, sank at the end of 1975, somewhere south of the Philippines. For over a fortnight, planes from the Japanese, Philippine and American air forces all searched the area from which her last radio message had been transmitted, to no avail. The day after the Americans called off their search, a Japanese fishing-boat found two survivors, two Spanish seamen, in a life-raft. One, Imeldo Leon, had been painting on deck when the ship was rocked by an explosion then sunk by two more only a few seconds later. He was flung into the water, clambered on to a life-raft and dragged an unconscious colleague with him. They were adrift for nineteen days, living off fish and rainwater before they were spotted.

Chance also played a part in the rescue of four crewmen from the *Flare**. Within twenty minutes of the alert being received a Hercules aircraft had taken off but started to search about thirty miles away from the ship's last known position. It took some hours before the pilot started to search over a

*See Chapter 2.

wider area and spotted part of a vessel that seemed to be torn in half. It turned out to be the 200-foot bow section of the *Flare*. With the water temperature at 2°C a human could be expected to survive for only four hours, so every minute was critical. A helicopter was dispatched but because of the weather it had been diverted from the position the crew had been given. They were trying to get back on track 'when we came across the oil slick on the water,' says Rob Butler, a flight engineer and winchman.

They decided to follow the slick. 'Obviously we were looking for a boat in trouble. We couldn't have gone any more than three or four miles and that's when I spotted a lifeboat, probably over a mile away. Once we closed in on it we saw people on top of it. It was upside down in the water. We could clearly see four people and they were in pretty bad shape. One fellow had started to wave after we circled once, and then after a couple of laps around the boat, three or four of them waved. It's a pretty good feeling to come across somebody in the middle of a huge expanse of water. They're on a lifeboat that's maybe 15 feet long and a needle in a haystack. It was just luck that we stumbled across them where they were, because they were not where we intended to start looking. They were probably five miles from the bow of the ship that had broken off and drifted away.'

Chris Brown, the pilot of the rescue helicopter, described how 'Six people had climbed on top of this lifeboat and about an hour before we arrived a wave had come over the top and knocked one of them off. He couldn't get back. It was too cold and you couldn't swim against the current. So he just floated off and they never saw him again. And then, a little while later, another was overcome by fatigue and slid off the side of the boat. One of the guys tried to hold him, but he just didn't have the strength to hold himself and this other guy next to the boat. And the other fellow couldn't climb back on, so he drifted away too. So the other four were just clinging on for dear life, and the waves were trying to knock them off. It was quite amazing that they survived.'

Under such conditions, a rescue requires a special combination of courage and cool professionalism. With the *Flare*, the rescuers had such a small target that they needed, says Rob Butler, 'to get over the lifeboat quickly, get the survivor or the SAR-tech* as close to the boat as we could and then back away. That way, we're not endangering the survivors on the

*Search-and-rescue technician.

lifeboat by blowing them off or blowing too much salt water up on them. We lowered him down until he was in the water from his knees down. Then we could taxi the helicopter forward to the target and try to put him down as close as we can. This was tricky because the boat's moving toward us and away from us 10 or 15 feet at a time, as well as up and down. So it's all a matter of timing and teamwork, between the front-end crew trying to interpret what I'm telling them to do, everybody setting up their own timing and the SAR-tech on the bottom of the hook trusting that he's going to get in there, not have to swim a mile to get to the boat.'

As Chris Brown says, 'I couldn't see the lifeboat, because it was basically under my feet at the time. So I had to depend on Master Corporal Butler to talk me over the top. It was a very tricky feat – we didn't have any auto-pilot.'

The first SAR-tech to launch himself overboard was Sergeant Tony Isaacs. He was lowered into the water as he approached the lifeboat and he swam with a hoist cable through the oil slick until he could grab the rope of the upturned boat and haul himself on to it. Swells of between 10 and 15 feet made hovering over the lifeboat difficult but eventually all four survivors were hoisted into the helicopter's rescue sling.

'Each and every one of the survivors came in the same condition,' Butler says. 'They were basically non-functional, they were staring at you, but you could tell that there wasn't a whole lot registering at this point. There's shock, they can't do anything for themselves. The rescue specialists will talk about the dangers of dealing with a hypothermic patient – you can't bump them and you have to be really careful when you're moving them around. On that day and in those conditions we knew we had only a short time to get these guys off the boat in the shape that they were in. When we were bringing them in we were being as gentle as we could, but we still had to be forceful.'

This was necessary with the final victim. He was rescued by the second SAR-tech, Paul Jackson, who took over because Isaacs was tired and was lowered from the helicopter. 'This was my first big rescue,' says Jackson, 'so it was new to me. I had never had to deal with anybody who wouldn't help me at all, he was so cold. By the time I got the sling around him and was ready to go up, I was getting a little tired myself, so we hoisted back up and I took the third guy up. I'll never forget the image of the fourth fellow we took up, and as I was ready to hoist the third guy, the fourth was grabbing on to my wetsuit and all that was going through my mind was hey, I got to get going and I will come back for you, and that's what I had said. But what was going through my mind as we were hoisting up was the fact that, for him, it's bad enough being out there with three other people, but to be the last one to be hoisted up must be worse.' So in that case, says Jackson, 'we got the third fellow up as quick as we could.'

'When we got back down to the last fellow,' he says, 'he didn't want to be left alone and his hand was up in the air, and he's indicating don't forget me, don't forget me. You could almost hear what he wanted to say. And you're fighting just to concentrate on what you're doing and put the emotion aside. And even our first officer, Captain Gough, said over the intercom, don't worry buddy, we're coming to get you.'

The last survivor 'actually ended up with a body temperature of 26.2°C, at 25°C your vital signs cease to exist. And he couldn't help me at all, and so I had to do everything for him. That took me a bit of time. I think the pilots lost a bit of a reference, and at one time I was almost hauled off the raft – I think I even had a cable wrapped round a flipper. But we got the last guy up into the helicopter, and we just started flying back for Saint Pierre, making a bee-line to the hospital. He was very combative the entire way. Sergeant Isaacs, he was the one who basically wrestled with him all the way back. With hypothermic patients we want them to move around as little as possible, so we felt it was in his best interest if we held him down, which we did. This is fairly common with people with a body temperature so low – that they go almost to a primitive state where they really don't know what they're doing. We tried to speak to him, but nothing was going in. We learned afterwards that he actually spoke the best English of all four of them. My job on the way back was to worry about the other three, and basically the only first-aid that we had time to do in the twenty-minute transit back was cutting off clothes, getting the survivors warm, and I was pretty happy when one of them asked for a smoke – then I knew he was coming round.' On the way back to base they saw the overturned lifeboat and two inflatable life-rafts but no more survivors. Even for the experienced Chris Brown this particular rescue 'will stick out in my mind because everything just happened so fast. We didn't know what to expect, and all of a sudden there were four guys, the only four left of a crew of twenty-five, and they were just so lucky to be alive and we were so happy to be there to help these guys. And especially in the hospital afterwards, the survivors saying thank you, my wife thanks you, my children thank you. I mean that really touches close to home, because you think of your own wife and children. That's quite, quite amazing.'

Even in waters warmer than those faced by the survivors from the *Flare*, the biggest danger is hypothermia. Dr Cameron Bangs, who specializes in 'cold injuries' ranging from frostbite to hypothermia, explains: 'The human body is designed to run at a certain temperature. We maintain that temperature by producing heat and by losing heat, and generally they stay in balance. When we're in an environment where we lose more heat than we can manufacture, our body temperature starts to drop. The body functions normally at a few degrees below normal, but once it reaches temperatures of 32°C then it does not function normally. We describe hypothermia as a temperature below 35°C. But there are two levels of hypothermia. If the core temperature or body temperature is below 32°C then that's profound hypothermia, and that can be lethal. If it's above that temperature people generally survive without any difficulty.'

In the non-lethal type, 'As we cool, the body tries to stay warm. It does so by shivering, by the teeth chattering. We try to get warm blood away from the skin so the warmth won't be lost. The skin turns pale, your lips turn blue and you'll appear cold.' Paradoxically, once you've descended into the dangerous levels, 'You stop shivering, your skin may actually get more blood flowing through and look better, so it's a difficult situation to try to recognize someone who's extremely cold. They look colder when they're actually warmer.'

The first thing that happens when you enter the water at, say, 11.1°C, a typical level for a cold sea, 'is that the cold stimulates your skin so that you increase your breathing, you gasp. If your face happens to be in the water you suck in large amounts of water and this, we think, causes the sudden-disappearance syndrome, where people fall into cold water and never come back up. After you gasp, you hyperventilate, experience intense discomfort, and have a panic feeling that you're doomed. As you stay in the water, three minutes, five minutes, the cold effect on the nerves in the hands and in the feet is such that they become extremely painful. The cold slows the conduction in the nerves so the muscles don't function. Someone who is in cold water for three minutes may not be able to help themselves get out – someone tosses them a rope, they may not be able to hold on to it, if they toss them a ladder they may not be able to climb up.'

The state of helplessness is well described by Matthew Sheahan, one of the survivors from the *Grimalkin* in the ill-fated 1979 Fastnet race*. As he points out, hypothermia is compounded by sheer physical exhaustion. 'One of the vivid memories I have is sitting in the cockpit, looking at my oilskin jacket, seeing it was undone and not being able to do anything about it. I knew it was undone, I knew it shouldn't be undone, but one of the effects of hypothermia is that your brain just comes to a grinding halt and, of course, that makes it worse.' But in the Irish Sea the biggest problem was not the cold. 'It was feeling tired and numb, dizzy and disorientated and, of course, that in itself doesn't help you control your boat in difficult situations.'

Normally, Dr Bangs reckons, 'At 11.1°C your body will maintain its normal temperature for thirty or forty minutes. When it starts to cool, you won't become severely hypothermic for an hour or an hour and fifteen minutes.' Yet Frosty Sloan, from the ill-fated *Cougar*† survived eighteen hours in the water. At first, he recalls, 'It wasn't super-cold when you first jumped in, but it *was* cold and it didn't take more than fifteen or twenty minutes before your hands started shaking and your jaws chattering. You had to clench your teeth together and it just progressively got worse. As you got colder you'd get cramps in your legs. I kept mine so that they pointed straight so that they wouldn't get more cramps. Pretty soon you just feel numb to the bone. I discovered fairly soon after getting in the water that if you kick and move your arms around you make the water circulate through your clothing and it is colder. If I kept my arms and legs together and didn't move about, I stayed warmer.

'One of the first things I kept trying to tell myself was to keep my mouth closed and not to get any salt water in it. Sometimes if I did I would try to gather up some saliva from somewhere and rinse my mouth out and then spit that out because I didn't want to get sick as other people were. I think once you start getting sick you go downhill that much quicker. That was the one thing that I concentrated on, and just trying to stay still.'

But then he realized that because the *Cougar*'s radio hadn't worked rescue was not at hand. 'I think, in a way, that helped keep me calm, because I didn't think that there was anything that I could do to make the

*See Chapter 12.
†See Chapter 7.

situation any better. When you accept your fate, it gives you a sense of calmness and you just go with it. Once I had realized that I wasn't going to make it, well I just started tidying up loose ends I guess you could say, and I spoke to each one of my children – I had three children at the time and a granddaughter that I call Bubba – and I just started saying goodbye.'

To make matters worse, the friend with whom Frosty had gone fishing had been sick all day. 'He was really in bad shape when we jumped into the water so I concentrated on trying to help him because he was having trouble keeping his face out of the water. Trying to reach across the life-ring and hold him up gave me something to do.'

Frosty developed bladder pressure: 'It was so cold and so painful that I couldn't urinate and I thought I was going to rupture from that as well as die from hypothermia. At one point I thought I was really starting to lose my mind because all of a sudden there was some light in the water and it was so bright that I could see my feet, but it was pitch dark and I thought, well, I'm really hallucinating now. And then the captain said, no, they were some kind of little phosphorous fish that glow real briefly and then they go away or they die. It gave the whole ocean scene an eerie feeling 'cause the waves would wash these fish up on the people that were alive, and the bodies that were in the water, so you could just see the glowing silhouettes of the bodies in the water.

'I was still awake. I was so cold I couldn't go to sleep, and when hypothermia started getting to the ones that died they would just start screaming. You couldn't really see them, but you could just hear these blood-curdling screams. It was like they were trying to talk but nothing was intelligible, it was just a bunch of words and symbols running together. Then they would just go quiet and that was the end. Each time each person went through that I thought what a very undignified way to die.

'A couple of times I just felt it would be so much easier to slip out of my life jacket and take a big gulp of water and get it over with, but I couldn't bring myself to do that. I'd just think about my kids and I couldn't do it.'

Dr Bangs believes that several factors contributed to Frosty's survival. His biggest asset was his size. 'Body fat keeps people warm . . . Second, he had on lots of clothing, which helped. Clothing traps water. Third, he had on a flotation device so he didn't have to tread water. He was also fortunate in the state of the sea. If you have big waves splashing over your head it cools you faster than if the sea is fairly calm. And he was able to hold still. The fastest way to die in cold water is to swim. You want to cuddle your body up, so that it won't move the water, and stay warm. The life jacket also held him up so he could get his body out of the water. The more your body is out of the water, the less heat you're going to lose. Fourth, he had a mental attitude. Some people just give up, but he didn't, although he thought of it.'

Rescue does not ensure survival, says Dr Bangs. 'A heart that has been cooled is like a mousetrap and if it is touched in the wrong way it will snap and go into ventricular fibrillation, in which it quivers and the person dies. Ventricular fibrillation is caused by exertion. I know of cases in which people have been floating in the water when someone rescues them and brings them to shore. They're allowed to walk, which pumps the cold blood from their legs back to the heart and they die of ventricular fibrillation and physical trauma. Rescuers need to know that if someone is found alive, they should remain alive unless they are jostled or handled roughly. Then they could fibrillate and die. Years ago the coastguard used to rescue people by dropping a rescue sling. They'd put the sling on and they'd pull them up this way and a lot of people died between the water and the helicopter. Now they use baskets to bring them up horizontally and they have much less of a problem.'

It is important to ensure that survivors are treated gently and no attempt is made to warm them too quickly or give them too much to eat or drink too soon. Frosty was warmed only gradually, but even so his heart muscles were damaged by the exertion. As the doctor described it to him, 'It is just like I'd tried lifting weights for eighteen hours. That's why my body was so sore and aching and my heart was worn out. I had to be slow and careful about my recovery, not overdo it and give my heart time to rest.'

Tony Bullimore recovered from his six-day ordeal sitting in the upturned hull of his yacht *Exide Challenger* after it had lost its keel in the lonely wastes of the southern Indian Ocean during a round-the-world race. His first reaction was that he could survive for a time because his boat, composed of watertight compartments, was not going to sink. Then, 'Bloody hell, I think – what a mess. At more than 50 degrees south, I'm over a thousand miles from the nearest shipping lanes. I'm at the arse-end of the world and couldn't be any further from rescue even if I tried.'*

Saved, Tony Bullimore, Little, Brown, London, 1997.

Inevitably, as time wore on, even he became depressed: 'Things are getting worse, not better. All the different contingencies I tried to put in place, none of them worked. I don't have any more ideas. I want to die doing something other than lying on a shelf. Let me wrestle with the helm, or bail out a life-raft, or trek across Antarctica, but don't let me die like this.'

But help was on the way. The signal from his Argos distress beacon had alerted the Australian Navy, and a frigate was steaming towards him. When it arrived, 'having travelled in hope, it had taken only one sighting of *Exide Challenger* to convince most watchers that it was a floating coffin rather than a safe haven'. Nevertheless, they dropped sonar buoys to try to trace any sound of human activity. The operator detected tapping but this could have been from many sources, like the rigging.

A copy of the tape was flown to John Postle, an expert trained to sift out human sounds from their noisy ocean background. 'When we listened to the tape,' Postle explains, 'we verified that there was a tapping sound that was different from the background noise. The first thing we did was listen to the tape at about a quarter speed, which enabled us to time the frequency of the noises accurately. What we heard there is that each successive sound was slightly different in its repetition rate, and what that told us was that it was probably not an electrical or mechanical noise.' From the timing of the sounds, Postle deduced that they didn't come from the rigging. The pattern was 'fairly characteristic of a pump. However it was unlikely to be a mechanically or electrically driven pump, due to the changing repetition rates. So, logically, the pump was more likely to be operated manually. It was probably going to be a fairly small pump, an osmosis pump, maybe, which turns saline water into fresh water for drinking. Listening to the sounds again, everything fitted, so we thought there was a survivor on board.'

The next day a rescue boat and divers went to the yacht and Bullimore swam out. His first reaction was, 'It's nice to be someone else's responsibility.' And then he told the coxswain of the rescue boat, 'I thought it time to make an appearance. If you didn't have a beard I'd kiss you.' And then, in sober retrospect: 'I wasn't brave. It was a horrific, traumatic experience. It was a case of praying and hoping that something was happening above the water. It was sheer determination, a little water, a little chocolate and hanging on in there, believing something might happen.'

14
Science to the Rescue

Someone has likened the amount of information that these systems provide as sort of trying to take a sip from a gushing fire hose.

Andrew Bowen

Maritime investigators have a long way to go before they can begin to compete with their fellow detectives in the world of air-crash detection. In the words of John Lang, chief inspector at the MAIB, their main problem is 'undoubtedly collecting evidence. Unlike the aviation industry, we rely very heavily on witnesses to tell us what occurred, but people's memories are fallible and very often we find that the evidence is conflicting, or contradictory, or incomplete. Other problems included [the fact that] there might be nothing there, the ship has sunk, we don't know where it is. Sometimes we have to wait quite a long time before something indicates her position. We've had one such incident in the last twelve months, a fishing-vessel called the *Marguerita Maria*. For four months nobody knew where she was. We do now and we're well on our way to identifying the causes of her sinking. Another fishing-vessel, which sank about three years ago, called *Provider*, hasn't been found, and although we can make a judgement as to why she was lost and, indeed, we've done so, we still don't 100 per cent know why it happened.'

Worse, 'In a collision situation where the other ship, whatever that might be, has vanished and we can't identify her, we are unable to proceed.'

Two recent investigations, on the bulk carriers *Derbyshire* and *Flare**, have shown that, with modern methods, an enormous amount can be done to find out what caused the death of a ship. For the first time, says Professor Douglas Faulkner, 'the *Derbyshire* investigation has come near to what the

*See Chapter 2.

aircraft people do. Most air accidents occur over land and they can examine every piece of the wreckage, bring it home and lay it out in a hangar. With a ship we've never had that luxury – nor, indeed, have people worried, providing the ship was insured. But I think that nowadays, anybody with a really important ship or a costly cargo who needs to understand why it was lost can use this technology to investigate. And because you can get really good-quality photographs from the seabed on the wreckage, then our situation is now nearly as good as that of the aircraft people.'

However, as Andrew Bowen, of the Woods Hole Institute of Oceanography in Massachusetts, who led the expedition to examine the wreck of the *Derbyshire*, points out: 'Working in extreme depths is a challenging environment for equipment to operate. The major difficulty is the tremendous pressures that are present in depths such as the *Derbyshire*; 4,200 metres is a long way down and all of the equipment has to be designed to resist those pressures. In addition to that there is the weather. We had to leave the survey site because of an approaching typhoon which, of course, had been responsible for the loss of the vessel in the first place.'

Their examination was 'multi-scale', ranging from location of the wreck down to the detailed examination of individual fractures. In this case, says Bowen, 'We were using high-definition television cameras to look at microscopic details of the wreckage. We deployed a side-scan system, which is an acoustic sensor, that gives us a very large view of the seabed' – including the distribution of the wreckage, all two thousand bits of it. 'The sonar was the first tool that we employed during the survey. The nice thing with the sonar is you don't need any underwater lighting; you can look through poor visibility. It helped us to find where the next step, which was using the Argo ROV vehicle, was to be employed. As opposed to the side-scan vehicle, the Jason ROV, the Argo generates high-altitude digital imagery from an altitude of approximately ten metres. And it was really the work-horse of the *Derbyshire* survey. We spent nearly three weeks over the wreckage site and collected 137,000 still digital images that covered the complete wreckage area in great detail.

Keeping track of these images was itself a major task. 'Each image that's gathered,' says Bowen, 'has attached to its digital file information about where the vehicle, in this case Argo, was. So we know precisely, within a few metres, where the photograph had been taken and from what altitude. That basic information, along with the image itself, was actually looked at four times on board the research vessel [by the investigatory team].'

Detailed navigation is a critical aspect. Not only do you have to be capable of manoeuvring the vehicle but you need to know where you've been. If you're looking for 100 per cent coverage, you have to know where each one of those photographs was taken so that you don't duplicate, and so that you're convinced that you've taken a picture of that particular part of the debris field. Data management in work like this is extremely important. Someone has suggested that using the amount of information that these systems provide is like trying to take a sip from a gushing fire-hose. You have to be really careful about being overwhelmed by the information, because if you can't organize it in a way that allows it to be interpreted then it's essentially useless.

'The vehicles have continuous video, which is transmitted in real time to the surface,' says Bowen. 'But images such as the mosaics rely on digital-imaging techniques. We have something that we call an electronic still camera. It takes a digital image, using strobe lights, of a much larger area than would be possible by just using a video camera. That digital image is then sent up the tether cable to the surface, where it's displayed and recorded and then available for the purposes such as mosaicing,' – assembling all the scraps of visual information into a coherent picture. Remember, says Bowen, 'Argo is suspended only ten metres above the sea floor. It gets a fairly small image on each of its photographs. So it takes many passes over an object to generate the imagery that can be linked together in the mosaicing process.'

In the case of the *Derbyshire*, a possible reason for the sinking had been structural failure. 'To gather information to allow interpretation for these purposes, we equipped the Jason ROV system with a high-definition television camera with a suitably equipped lens that allowed macro photography.' They could then take high-definition pictures of the potential weak spots to show how the ship's plates actually fractured.

But none of this information would be usable if it could not be transmitted to the surface, which requires fibre optics. 'The tether cable that attaches Jason to the surface ship is over nine kilometres long at its full length. And it would be impossible to transmit high-quality imagery over a copper cable. Just as telecommunications have been revolutionized through the use of fibre optics, so has exploration of the deep sea.'

Fortunately, the investigators had not lost sight of the real loss involved in the sinking of the *Derbyshire*: the death of forty-four people. 'Before leaving the site we conducted a brief memorial service. I think all of us, at times, during the course of the survey, felt a certain affinity for those lost. And I think it's fair to say that a lot of the effort we put into that work was done in their name. And certainly we all hope that the outcome of this work ultimately is a legacy from those who were lost, which will help to improve the safety of vessels in general.' For, Bowen believes, 'The survey of the *Derbyshire* was an important step forward for our capabilities, specifically with regard to management of large volumes of information, and the nature of that information being multi-scale, from the very large to the very small. In 1997 they used the same equipment in the same way in the Mediterranean to look at a wreck that was lost in the fourth century AD, a Roman trading vessel.' Bowen insists, 'These techniques are extremely appropriate for scientific endeavour, and not only for marine-accident investigations, but for people trying to understand things about the environment. Having this type of capability in deep ocean is of profound importance in terms of increasing our understanding.'

ROVs, like the Argo, are the key to much of the improvement in undersea investigation. They can be used as the platform for video and still cameras, but also – in waters shallower than those in which the *Derbyshire* sank – they can use manipulator arms to retrieve pieces from wreckage. The Canadians, says John Garstang, an investigator with the country's Transportation Safety Board, have already had several successes. 'We lost a fishing-vessel in the Gulf of St Lawrence several years ago. It was called the *Nadin*, and it was sitting on the bottom in about 70 feet of water. We used an ROV and some divers to have a look and we were able to determine one of the main reasons why it sank. Eventually the wreck was salvaged and brought to the surface, but we had the information long before this happened. We also lost a tug in fairly deep water in bad weather and we didn't know what had happened to her, the EPIRB [emergency position indicating radio beacon] did not go off, and we knew she had one. But we were able to find the wreck and dived on it using ROVs. We found a large hole in the bow, which we had not been privy to before then. There were no survivors from that wreck, so it would have been difficult to determine just what had happened without the technology that we were able to use.'

Other devices used by investigators include an underwater acoustic homing system described by Garstang as 'a cylindrical object that can be mounted on the underwater vehicle; it's basically an underwater microphone, called a hydrophone. If we see some wreckage of significance that we need to mark for subsequent retrieval, we can mark it with a beacon and that device is used to home in on the beacon.' Radar pictures can also help. In the case of the *Flare*, pictures from satellites show 'a bright return that is the vessel itself, but also of interest are some lines extending off the vessel itself, which is its wake. This may provide valuable evidence to us on the condition of the vessel prior to the occurrence. We might be able to get heading and speed by analysing the size and pattern of the wake, knowing the shape of the hull. The imagery may also give us information such as the sea state, wind direction, what the vessel is doing, is it dead in the water, is it transiting.'

On the *Flare*, the ROV, Garstang says, is being used 'to look at a variety of things. One is, of course, the fracture surfaces themselves. We'll be inspecting for possible cracks, there may be fatigue. And we also use the vehicle to inspect intact sections of the hull, to see its type of construction. We have blueprints that give us information, but there's the theoretical and then there's the actual. The ROV will allow us to look at welds or bulkheads or patterns – paint patterns, rust patterns, if there was a fire, smoke or soot patterns, if they exist. So we'll be doing the inspection visually, but also we'll be utilizing the sonar to examine areas that possibly we may not be able to see because of limited visibility, or that are beyond the field of view from our underwater lights. The vehicle is also equipped with a 3-D profiler, which is similar in concept to sonar. Basically this will immediately give us similar information underwater from the ROV vehicle itself.'

In the future it may even be possible to send a man down at least to depths of a thousand feet, using a 'newt-suit'. This, says Garstang, 'is basically the concept of a space suit, where the diver is in a one-atmosphere environment or, in other words, in a room-pressure environment, and can fly himself around in his newt-suit. This newt-suit has the advantage that, with an individual under water, we have a little more dexterity: a manned operator can do things that a vehicle can't, in certain situations.'

The science-fiction equipment has already proved useful. 'In March 1993,' says Garstang, 'what was referred to as the Storm of the Century occurred. A ship called the *Goldborne Conveyor* was approximately a hundred miles off Nova Scotia. The captain eventually put out a call indicating he was taking on water, but for an unknown reason. The Canadian Department of National Defence Search and Rescue dispatched an Aurora patrol aircraft. It orbited the scene and took FLIR pictures [forward-looking infrared], which is video imagery, but in the infrared band, so that in very low light and poor weather conditions you can see better than you could by conventional vision. The aircraft also took conventional photographic imagery, vertical, with a photo-flash unit. The FLIR imagery was subsequently shown on the national news, showing the vessel floundering then eventually sinking. And the answer, or potential answer, as to why the vessel sank was visible in the FLIR imagery that was aired publicly.

'Although the imagery had been examined by a variety of people and nothing out of the ordinary was detected, one of our marine investigators took the initiative to send it to us for computer image-processing work [in which] we take the imagery and we digitize it. Once in the computer, we can do several different types of mathematical operation to manipulate the image to try to enhance detail.' As a result, 'The FLIR imagery showed that a couple of doors at the stern of the vessel were open, doors that were used to allow a conveyor belt to come out for loading and unloading purposes. The vessel was carrying a full load of gypsum. We were able to show that the rear doors were open and the assembly for the conveyor belt was dragging in the water, leaving a wake. By studying the dimensions of the door arrangement and the height of the door-sill, we could show that the fact that the assembly was dragging in the water, menat that water was in fact above the level of the door-sill, therefore would be free to flow into the vessel itself.

'Inspection was done on a sister ship, and it was discovered that when the side door is also open, that conveyor belt transfers material to another conveyor belt which basically runs the length of the ship to the various holds. There are no watertight doors along that conveyor-belt system. The indications that we had from the analysis were that, with the heavy weather, the *Goldborne Conveyor* was trimmed bow-end down to weather the storm. Our data showed that, with the doors open, water was entering the conveyor system. It's consistent that water flowing downhill would flow down the conveyor tunnel towards the bow and fill it. This, and our analysis of the imagery, was consistent with that type of scenario because the vessel was slowly taking on water, sinking further and listing, until eventually it was observed that a wave of 100 to 125 feet went over the bow right back and over the bridge. The aircraft was just passing in some low cloud or fog and lost sight of the *Goldborne Conveyor*, but when it came back on another pass to keep station with the ship, the ship had disappeared. All thirty-three on board died.

'We were able to detect something that was already out there that other people didn't see. With the computer we're able to take an image that is sometimes fuzzy or blurred and enhance it, making it clearer or bringing out finer detail. And that's basically what we did with the FLIR imagery. We were able to show that the doors were open. Then the question came, well, maybe the doors were open because the crew elected to egress out of those doors. We went back to the Department of National Defence records and were able to get a time-line of a sequence of different FLIR shots of the ship, to show that the doors were most probably open for a considerable period of time, that this wasn't just damage done while it was sinking.'

They also did a vision analysis. 'From the bridge, could the crew see that the loading doors were open near the stern? And based on the imagery we had, studying view angles, our determination was no, they couldn't, that the only way these doors could be observed to be open, other than going to that location internally, was to go out on the wing. And, of course, since they were in the Storm of the Century, that wasn't a possibility. Since they could see their bow sinking slowly and they were taking on water, the crew may have perceived that the problem was in fact forward, not aft. Also, working with our regional office who inspected the sister ship, we discovered that there were no warning alarms, should the doors come open, to notify the crew that they had become unlatched or battered by the seas. Evidence started to form that there could be a safety concern on the integrity of the doors, the way they were designed.

'One of our marine investigators, who boarded a sister ship, studied the tunnel system and found that the bilge-pumping system works fine if the vessel is trimmed back towards the stern, but as soon as it's trimmed, say in bad weather with the bow down, and as soon as the tunnel fills with water, you cannot get at the valves for the bilge-pumping system in the tunnel network. This was another major finding, because if this scenario is going on, where water is entering through the open doors, and flooding down forward, and the crew does not realize where it's coming from, even if they had anyone who could go to the tunnel area they could not get the bilge systems tunnels to pump out because of the location of the valves.'

Not all the equipment is specially devised for maritime investigation. In the lab they use freeze-drying equipment on the precious documents recovered from a wreck. As a Canadian technician explains: 'Freeze-drying is a sublimation process whereby you go from a solid state to a gaseous state. The water is converted directly from solid ice into gas. That process reconstitutes the paper and allows us to restore the documents to almost original condition. We recovered some from the body of the chief officer of the *Flare*.' When they had pieced together the fragments, they found they had a description of how to calculate currents. 'Also from the chief officer, we recovered a throat-lozenge wrapper. From information like this we can determine how the person was feeling, and if he had to write down notes on how to calculate currents, that he wasn't knowledgeable in that area. A complete crew list was also recovered, and various pieces of scrap paper on which were written co-ordinates and dates. From examining the course of the ship we can get a good idea of where it was on these dates. Another document is a record of fuel consumption from a previous trip, from a port in the Caribbean to Rotterdam. With this we can get a pretty good estimate of how much fuel is still on board the ship underwater.'

With other equipment the Canadians can reconstruct a vessel in 3D on a screen and use the information gleaned from an underwater survey to work out crucial information such as the position of the lifeboats and whether they could have been launched. The Canadians also have a 3D human-modelling machine which can tell, for instance, if the victims were wearing immersion suits. 'Combined with the underwater vehicle, this may enable us to look at those details on the stern section, for example. Were there immersion suits? Are they there? If they're stowed somewhere, are they accessible?'

When it comes to studying injuries, 'by using these types of models it's very easy to visualize, because we can colour-code different injury types. Just seeing helps the whole team to understand better what occurs. The pathologists working with us on the body models found it a great tool as well.' They can be used to check on the state of individual body organs: 'If by chance,' says Garstang, 'there is a fire on board, sometimes the victims inhale the smoke and soot patterns are left within the trachea and in the lungs. Using the computer model we could colour-code areas that show signs of unique damage related to, say, a fire explosion. Similarly, if an individual has been exposed to a blast, there are certain pressure effects that you may see, such as broken eardrums, embolisms in the lung. Similarly certain tissue samples, whether from the liver or elsewhere in the body, may reveal the presence of certain chemicals that may be significant, such as the by-products of smoke or fire. For instance, if you were to burn certain types of plastic, you might get hydrogen cyanide or hydrogen fluoride, or you might get carbon monoxide.'

The Canadians can also reconstruct what the crew on the bridge saw at the time of the disaster – what the scientists call bridge-situational aware-ness. 'You have to try to reconstruct what other people perceived at the time of the occurrence,' says Garstang. 'To do that we may want to use body models to reposition the individuals on the bridge and look through their eyes to see what they saw, which might explain why certain people acted in certain ways. One individual may have seen something and interpreted it differently from another. That may be related to his field of view, to prob-lems such as glare, reflections, perception in lighting, colour patterns, things of that nature. The body models allow us to run permutations and combi-nations again. What if the individual was here and was looking that way? We can actually reconstruct things and run them through different combina-tions to assist the investigation team on trying to [get a] basic understand-ing of why somebody might have done something. It may have been that their perception was totally different from another person's.

'We also have a human-performance section within the organization. These people are psychologists, and they're able to help with the investiga-tion of individuals, what made someone tick, what made him, perhaps, make a mistake where he's done everything correctly in the past. This is all new stuff to us, which we never had in the seventies and eighties. We're able to produce documents now that are much more complete, that the public are happier to read, because we're able to determine cause much more easily than we used to.'

But none of these scientific advances can be truly effective without inter-national agreement, and this is slow in coming, even when it concerns the compulsory installation of devices that all the investigators agree are of cru-cial importance to safety. Top of the list comes the marine equivalent of the black box, the flight-deck recorder and cockpit voice recorder installed for decades in every commercial aircraft in the world. 'A Voyage Data Recorder,' says Eric Snow, investigator with the Canadian Safety Board 'could either be a float-free unit or a unit that would go down with the ship but have a beacon on it so that we'll be able to find it. It would beep for several hours. It would record on a regular basis many important parame-ters aboard that ship – stresses on the hull, the weather being recorded at the time, the engine revs – which would be invaluable to the investigator should that vessel sink and we're able to recover it.'

To John Lang of the MAIB: 'The one thing I dream about is having the voyage data recorder widely fitted. Progress has been made through the IMO [International Maritime Organization], but we haven't got there yet. Other countries have reservations about the extent of the fitting and what should feature in the recorder itself. But if I had that, it would transform my ability to get to the bottom, remove a lot of the inconsistencies and the conflicting evidence which we're currently faced with.'

But even a black box will have limits in a maritime setting. As Captain Paul Esbensen of the NTSB (National Transportation Safety Board) points out, it would be most useful in recording not voices but data. 'Data recorders have their limitations. If you start to restrict them to the conversations on a four-hour watch on the bridge like that, I don't think you'll gain enough from them. I think the data recorders are the best things you have as far as ship speed, heading, rudder angle indicators, helm orders, ship's systems go, or to register how much the ship rolls, how much she pitches, the rough weather, the wind and everything else. All that can be put on the recorder easily and they can develop enough out of that without listening to what was going on up there.'

The black box is not the only device that could be useful. 'We talk sometimes about automatic indicator systems,' says John Lang, 'whereby there's a transponder, which would be of less value to me but which could be extremely useful in, say, a collision situation where external radar coverage has been provided – typically within the Dover Strait.' James Dickson, who was deeply involved in attempts to prevent the tanker *Braer* from hitting the rocks of the Shetland Islands, is perplexed that the transponder is not a compulsory fitting. 'It's extremely cheap, the technology's there, so we can't understand why it's taken so long to fit transponders. They will tell you the ship, its name, where it is, how fast it's going, et cetera, et cetera. Aircraft have them, lorries have them, taxis have them. They all bounce the signals off satellites and it's extremely cheap. It would be a big help to us to see what ships were in the vicinity and what they were doing.' In the case of the *Braer*: 'No one knew she had broken down until the master got on the VHF, which was some considerable time after he got into trouble.'

Lang also mentions the EPIRB (emergency positioning indicator radio beacon). 'That's the electronic speaker that transmits in the event of a ship sinking. It will help us locate vessels that otherwise sink without trace. It is now widely fitted though sadly, too often, it doesn't function and that is a worry. We're trying to get to the bottom of that one as well.' Andy Liddell, a survivor from the *Cougar** laments that the boat did not have EPIRB which 'would have picked us up by satellite. Planes also can pick up the transmission they put out and they would have found us. We may have spent only an hour or two in the water. Unfortunately that vessel did not have one because we were carrying fewer than seven [passengers]. We could sail up to fifty miles offshore and we were not required to have an EPIRB. The coastguard regulations have changed since then, and more boats are required to carry an EPIRB.'

The list of seemingly obvious ways to prevent accidents and to preserve life is endless. Richard Johnson of the NTSB is particularly unhappy with 'the sort of life-float found on the *Cougar,* which is designed just to hold your head above water'. This, as he says, 'does not have sufficient buoyancy to allow people to get inside it'. It is far better to have 'an inflatable buoyant apparatus, which allows people who are forced to get into the water [to get inside it, and it] will protect them from immersion in water and also from the effects of hypothermia.'

But the endlessness of the list should not prevent progress. The safety convoy clearly cannot continue sailing at the speed of the slowest vessel.

*See Chapter 7.

Index